Abdullah Mubarak Al-Sabah

Abdullah Mubarak Al-Sabah

The Transformation of Kuwait

By Souad M. Al-Sabah

I.B. TAURIS

LONDON · NEW YORK

ALS

Published in 2015 by I.B.Tauris & Co. Ltd
www.ibtauris.com

Distributed worldwide by I.B.Tauris & Co Ltd
Registered office: 6 Salem Road, London W2 4BU

ISBN: 978 1 78076 433 7
eISBN: 978 0 85773 852 3

A full CIP record for this book is available from the British Library
A full CIP record is available from the Library of Congress

Library of Congress Catalog Card Number: available

Typeset by Data Standards Ltd, Frome, Somerset
Printed and bound in Great Britain by T.J. International, Padstow,
Cornwall

MIX
Paper from
responsible sources
FSC® C013056

S A

Table of Contents

List of Plates

9   At Kuwait Airport for the first Kuwait Airlines flight, March
     1954.

10   Sheikh Abdullah Mubarak receiving the first class of Kuwaiti
     pilots after their graduation from the United Kingdom, 1954.

11   Sheikh Abdullah Mubarak as Commander-in-Chief of the
     Kuwaiti Armed Forces.

12   A live ammunition manoeuvre with his officers.

13   At the official ceremony celebrating the coming to power of
     Sheikh Abdullah Salem Al-Sabah as Emir of Kuwait, 1950.

14   Sheikh Abdullah Al Salem and Sheikh Abdullah Mubarak
     drinking a cup of water at Kuwait's first desalination plant,
     Shuwaikh, March 1953.

15   Presidents Gamal Abdel Nasser of Egypt and Choukri Al-
     Kouatli of Syria visiting Sheikh Abdullah Mubarak at his
     Alexandria house in 1958. Anwar Al-Sadat and Abdel
     Hakim Amer appear in the picture.

16   Sheikh Abdullah Mubarak at his last official function during
     the visit of King Saud of Saudi Arabia, April 1961.

17   Sheikh Abdullah Mubarak inspecting the Kuwaiti police
     force in 1959.

18   At the wedding of Mona Gamal Abdel Nasser with his wife,
     Souad Al-Sabah, and first son Mubarak in 1965.

19   Sheikh Abdullah Mubarak receiving Sheikh Hamad, the
     Emir of Bahrain, 1958.

20   Examining the Ahmadi oilfields in 1949 with Abdullah Al-
     Mulla, Government Secretary, Sir Phillip Southwell,
     Managing Director of the Kuwait Oil Company (on his left)
     and Mr L. T. Jordan, General Manager of the Kuwait Oil
     Company.

21   Receiving King Mohammed V of Morocco in 1960.

22   Receiving Prince Faisal, the Crown Prince of Iraq, in Kuwait,
     mid-1950s.

Preface

The inspiration for this book came to my mind in the aftermath of the Iraqi invasion of Kuwait in 1990. The occupation authorities declared Kuwait to be the '19th province of Iraq' and its political autonomy was denied. The destruction that ensued during the occupation was accompanied by an almost systematic campaign of pillage and plunder throughout most areas of Kuwait.

The ordeal left a lasting impact on my thinking. It brought home to me the importance of documenting the modern history of my country, which I felt as a sort of moral and ethical duty. I was an insider to many events that I thought should be brought to light. However, this book is not a compilation of personal memories and recollections. I studied carefully almost all previous works in Arabic and English on Kuwait during the lifetime of Sheikh Abdullah Mubarak Al-Sabah and I interviewed a lot of people who worked with him or served under his command. I also researched British, American and Kuwaiti archives. The first edition of this book appeared in 1995. After five reprints and three editions in Arabic, I thought it should be made available to a Western audience.

The book focuses on the life and history of Sheikh Abdullah Mubarak Al-Sabah, who was a prominent Kuwaiti statesman. He served as Deputy Ruler of Kuwait during most of the 1950s until his resignation in 1961. These times were characterized by rapid social change; a traditional society was shaken from its roots under the impact of the newly founded oil wealth – and the foundations of modern and independent Kuwait were laid during that decade. The book analyses the role of Abdullah Mubarak in the context of a changing Kuwait. I believe that the quality of leadership makes a difference, especially in times of turmoil and uncertainty. I have tried to underline the role of the Sheikh in dealing with the accelerated changes that swept Kuwait in all walks of life during that period. At times he managed the changes well, at other times he initiated the changes, and at others he steered Kuwait and its people into a safe haven.

I thank all my friends in Kuwait, Cairo and London who helped me in the preparation of this study. Their continuous help and support were essential in order to complete the work.

I hope that this book will be useful to all those who seek to understand the modern history of Kuwait.

Souad Al-Sabah
Kuwait, October 2014

Introduction

This book describes the history and life of the prominent Kuwaiti statesman Sheikh Abdullah Mubarak Al-Sabah, whose contribution was instrumental to the founding of a modern independent Kuwait.

The strength of his role stemmed from three major sources. First, he enjoyed distinguished status within the ruling Al-Sabah family – he was the only living son of Sheikh Mubarak the Great (Mubarak Al-Kabir), the founder of the state (reigned 1896–1915). Thus, he was 'uncle' of all rulers and dignitaries of Kuwait from 1915 onwards.

Second, over the years, Abdullah Mubarak was trained in different administrative, security and political positions. When he was 14 years old he was tasked with administering one of the 'gates' of Kuwait: at that time the city was surrounded by a number of gates that were kept open during daylight and closed by night. Abdullah Mubarak fought smuggling, protected borders and preserved law and order in the desert separating Kuwait from Iraq. The book records many details about his role and responsibilities.

Third, in the 1950s he assumed the position of Deputy Ruler and developed excellent working relations with the ruling sheikh (who was in fact his elder nephew, Sheikh Abdullah Al-Salem), for whom he acted as trusted right-hand man.

The significance of Abdullah Mubarak's life can best be appreciated against the context of social and economic change that took place in Kuwait from the late 1940s onwards.

From traditionalism to modernity

During the first four decades of the twentieth century, life in Kuwait was generally traditional and simple. Kuwait was relatively open to the outside world due to its strategic position, its tradition of pearl fishing and its commercial links to India. Nevertheless, its people maintained Kuwait's traditional mode of economy, politics and culture.

The discovery of oil and the export of the first cargo in 1946 upturned this traditional equilibrium. All aspects of society started to undergo fundamental and rapid change as a result. Thousands of people of different nationalities, ethnicities and religions flocked into the country searching for work and to settle. Kuwaiti culture and ways of conducting life were now subject to external influences. At the same time, the Kuwaiti Government recognized the importance of education and sent missions of young people to study at universities in Egypt and Iraq.

In the 1950s, change permeated the whole of Kuwaiti society. New roads were built and modern buildings were constructed. Schools were opened and for the first time Kuwaiti girls were able to enrol. Cars, electrical appliances and home equipment became popular among Kuwaiti families.

Transitional periods are, by definition, difficult times. This was even more true in the case of Kuwait because of the tempo and scope of change there. Abdullah Mubarak occupied a senior position among the Kuwaiti ruling elite who were in charge of managing and steering that process of change.

Although Abdullah Mubarak grew up in the desert and maintained great respect for Bedouin culture and traditions, he nevertheless understood the needs of the changing times. Rather than resist change he saw the opportunities to be gained. A new, better world was opening up and Kuwait had a part to play in it.

This book demonstrates how the Sheikh was a pioneer in accepting new ideas and ways of doing things. For instance, in the face of opposition he spoke out to encourage girls' education and initiated the plan to establish a Kuwaiti university. He encouraged young people to enjoy modern sports and was a patron of many educational incentives such as school athletics competitions.

On a personal level he was open-minded. This is reflected in his family life. His wife pursued a university education at Cairo and Surrey universities and she became the first Kuwaiti woman to hold a PhD in economics. Not only that, but since she was also a poet, he encouraged her to make public appearances in Kuwait and abroad to recite her poetry. The same was true with the rest of our family; he was committed to offering us the best education available.

Institution-building

Abdullah Mubarak built institutions. He understood that institutions guaranteed continuity and endurance because they outlive individuals. For this reason the book explains in detail his role in areas such as security, the army, civil aviation, education, broadcasting and non-governmental associations.

His most lasting influence was in the area of security and the military. Entrusted with various security responsibilities during World War II, he was decorated by the British Government in

1945. Before independence, he perceived the threats to Kuwaiti national security and the importance of establishing a strong army for his country. He subsequently laid the foundation of the Department of Public Security, which later became the army of Kuwait. This book shows the challenging negotiations he held with the British Government to acquire new advanced weapons.

Similarly, he took a keen interest in civil aviation and, realizing its importance, he established a club to encourage the young people of Kuwait in this activity. He foresaw the importance of training Kuwaitis as civil pilots as a preliminary step for their military role. In the same vein, he started to modernize and expand Kuwait's airport and to establish a national airline.

Quest for independence

In 1899, Sheikh Mubarak Al-Sabah signed a treaty with the British Government, according to which Kuwait became a British protectorate. London was responsible for conducting Kuwait's foreign affairs, while domestic matters were the domain of the Kuwaiti Emir. The British appointed a 'Political Agent' to act as their diplomatic representative. In many cases, the Political Agent went beyond his jurisdiction, which created frictions with the Emir.

Abdullah Mubarak understood the importance of maintaining the link with Great Britain as a counterbalance to Iraqi territorial ambitions in Kuwait. At the same time he was a patriot who opposed British intervention in the domestic affairs of his country. This book considers the difficulties inherent in keeping a balance between the two and, in this, relates many examples that touch on his assertion of Kuwaiti autonomy.

For example, in the late 1940s, he ordered the entry of Arab citizens into Kuwait without a visa and accepted a Lebanese medal without the prior consent of the British Government. As a result, his relations with the British were ambivalent. On the one side, the British authorities admired his strong personality, which was a guarantee for order and stability against subversive activities. On the other side, they disapproved of his support of Nasser's Egypt and the Algerian revolution. They were equally puzzled by his call in 1958 for Kuwait to join the League of Arab States, three years before independence.

Political succession

British diplomatic correspondence is full of accounts and rumours about conflict within the Sabah family over the political succession. When Sheikh Ahmed Al-Jaber passed away in 1950 while his heir Sheikh Abdullah Al-Salem was abroad, the Political Agent wrote about different scenarios including the possibility of having a coup engineered by Sheikh Abdullah Mubarak. The book records all the details of this incident and shows that these scenarios were entirely fictitious and had no basis in reality.

Throughout the 1950s, Political Agents' reports frequently referred to the political ambitions of Abdullah Mubarak and cast doubt on his plans and intentions. Yet, as will be explored throughout this book, the accounts made in these reports were often motivated by suspicion as to his stance on, in particular, the communist activities at that time. Although Abdullah Mubarak held all the instruments of military power, he never used them as a card in domestic politics. As an example of this, when he disagreed with the Emir in 1960 on a number of policy issues he resigned and left the country quietly. For the following

31 years, he observed Kuwaiti politics, gave his advice when sought and supported Kuwaiti and Arab causes to the best of his abilities.

This book tells the story of his life and work, as a statesman who practised politics in difficult and changing times. It is to his credit that he helped to bring about the development, independence and stability of Kuwait today.

~1~

Abdullah Mubarak:
The Formative Years

S heikh Abdullah Mubarak Al-Sabah was the youngest son of Sheikh Mubarak Al-Sabah, the founder of modern Kuwait who was known as Mubarak the Great by his contemporaries. Between his accession in 1896 and his death in 1915, Sheikh Mubarak Al-Sabah created a secure future for a small state sandwiched between two large and powerful neighbours, the future Saudi Arabia and the future Iraq. His youngest son, Abdullah Mubarak Al-Sabah, the subject of this book, was born in 1914, a year before his father died, and went through life with no personal recollection of him. Whatever he knew of his father he acquired through his branch of the Al-Sabah family and other contemporaries who knew his father and his remarkable career at first hand. Only one of his older brothers, Hamad, born in 1894, lived long enough to pass on memories of their father. Yet Abdullah Mubarak idolized his father, and the evidence of his political life clearly shows that the youngest son made sustained and determined efforts to follow the causes that had been central to his father's life.

Sheikh Mubarak Al-Sabah was a pioneer in his ideas of Arab identity, although, perforce, the Ruler of Kuwait had to remain on good terms with the Ottoman rulers to the north, with the intent of keeping any Ottoman involvement in Kuwait at arm's length. At the end of World War I, all dimensions of politics had altered in Kuwait. The Ottoman Empire had ceased to function, and the British became the unquestioned and dominant imperial presence in the region. The British took no more benign a view of Arabism than the Ottomans had done, yet in pursuing this political course in the decades that followed, Abdullah Mubarak would have an easier task than his father. Sheikh Mubarak Al-Sabah had been compelled to maintain Kuwait's independence by juggling relations with the British and the Ottomans: Abdullah Mubarak never had this complex double task. He had only to confront a determined and powerful British administration, even if this was ultimately less malleable than its Ottoman predecessors.

After his father's death, the infant Abdullah Mubarak was in an anomalous position. The new Ruler of Kuwait was his elder brother, Jaber II, who was born in 1860. Sheikh Jaber died in 1917 and his younger brother Salem II (born in 1864) succeeded him. Yet he had only a brief period of power, dying in 1921. By 1921, only two of Sheikh Mubarak Al-Sabah's sons were still alive: Hamad, by then 24, and the seven-year-old Abdullah Mubarak. Kuwait was under threat from many enemies, and a young and inexperienced ruler could have been disastrous. The Al-Sabah family took much less account of heredity than weightier considerations: who would be the most effective ruler? Neither an inexperienced young man (Hamad) nor a minor (Abdullah Mubarak) would do. Thus the succession passed to the elder son of Jaber, Ahmed II, the nephew of Abdullah Mubarak, but nonetheless more than 35 years his senior. Ahmed II ruled Kuwait for more than 30 years until 1950. On his death, his cousin Abdullah III (the elder son of Salem II) ruled until 1965, when his brother Sabah III succeeded, and ruled until 1977. At that point, the succession returned to the other main branch of the family, to the grandson of Jaber II, who ruled as Jaber III until 2006.

In this complex pattern of dynastic movement, Abdullah Mubarak's position was unique. He was (after Hamad's death in 1938) the sole surviving son of the founder of the nation; he also seemed to have inherited his father's talents. His own family quietly noted his acute political sense and determination, as well as his dedication to both the nation and the Arab cause.

In understanding Abdullah Mubarak's career, both his personal, family background and the nature of change in Kuwait are of equal importance. For over half a century after 1940 Sheikh Abdullah Mubarak was either Deputy Ruler at the heart of Kuwait's political life, or, when out of office, a loyal supporter of both the Kuwaiti people and the ruling family. He was an eyewitness to many momentous events; and contributed to the making of many others. He came to know the leading Arab and foreign politicians and statesmen, as well as kings, presidents and senior officials; in his long career, he became completely at home with the challenging complexities of Arab politics. Like his father, he believed intuitively in the ideals of Arabism, becoming over time a powerful and effective advocate for those ideals, which were central to Kuwait's development during the 1940s and 1950s.

§

In this period, Abdullah Mubarak tackled energetically the problems of Kuwait's relative underdevelopment; yet in British records of the period, we see mostly distrust of him and his assumed motives. There were few local records (other than the press) or Arab memoirs to provide a corrective of Kuwait at that time. Thus, we have no alternative but to use the comprehensive records held in the British National Archives in London and the US National Archives in Maryland. Both, however, need to be used with great care. The early reports were often based on gossip and self-interested hearsay, at least until 1904 when British officials were first based in Kuwait and could judge events at first hand. However, even after 1904 British officials were in no sense independent observers of any matter that touched the political and economic interests of the United Kingdom. It is a measure of how highly successive governments in London rated the importance of Kuwait that so tight a control was imposed upon the small emirate.

The signing of an oil concession agreement in 1934, and the first discovery of oil in 1938, marked Britain's increasing interest in Kuwait: the contract was with a company jointly owned by the US Gulf Corporation and the Anglo-Persian Oil Company, which took the name British Petroleum in 1954. On 30 June 1946, when Sheikh Ahmed al-Jaber Al-Sabah, the Ruler of Kuwait, turned the wheel that started the flow of Kuwait's first crude oil into the holding tanks aboard the tanker *British Fusilier*, the transformation of Kuwait's economy became possible. However, it came at the price of an even more insistent British determination to exercise greater control.

Abdullah Mubarak was born into a society taking the first steps towards modernity. During his long life he played many different roles that consolidated this process. Generations of British officials in Kuwait recognized that he was incorruptible, diligent, self-willed, single-minded and unusually well-informed. All these qualities made him a potential threat, but most dangerous of all was that as a senior member of the ruling family he carried real authority: he could not be marginalized or overruled as could lower ranks of officialdom. It is remarkable how far his influence and experience extended. He directed public security and the Police Department, founded Kuwait's army, established civil aviation, supervised the Council of Education, radio and passports. More than any other member of the ruling family, he understood in detail – and in practice – how Kuwaiti society functioned.

We know tantalizingly little about his childhood and even less about his development before he first appears in the British reports from Kuwait. Abdullah Mubarak spent his early childhood years entirely within the Bedouin structure of life and traditions. The tribes of the Arabian Peninsula shared a common heritage and social ethics, but the opportunities offered by the Gulf for fishing and, later, pearling, meant that a number of tribes led a 'double life' according to the season. Kuwait looked both outward to the Gulf and maritime trade, whilst also northward into modern Iraq. The great scholar of the Bedouin, Jibrail S. Jabbur, points out that while not all Arabs lived off the desert, it was the land in which they were formed: 'The traditional life of the Arabs had strong roots in nomadism; and even today the Arab sedentary mentality is firmly bonded to that of the Arab Bedouin ... The Arab does not know himself or understand his unique qualities and the range of his capacity for development, if he does not know that the way that he lives has its roots in the desert.' [Jabbur]

In the case of Abdullah Mubarak, his sense of the tribal spirit, deep need for family solidarity, and even his desire for positions of authority and leadership, can be traced back to the influence of Bedouin life. He grew up as a Bedouin. After his father's death he was cared for by his 'milk mother', 'Nuwair', wife of Mutlaq Abu Hadida, who at the same time nursed her own daughter, Haya. According to prevailing custom, the Abu Hadida family of the Al-Rashaida tribe took him to grow up in the desert. Haya became his 'milk sister', which constituted a powerful connection in Bedouin society. The best Western writer on Kuwait, H. R. P. Dickson, described how he experienced a similar kind of childhood: 'Firstly, I was wet-nursed by an Anizah woman of the Misrab section of the Ruwala [Bedouin] and can claim milk-brotherhood with them. Secondly, the fact that I have spoken Arabic from childhood.'[1] Dickson learned the hidden and often unspoken aspects of Bedouin culture, and his analysis gives us a powerful insight into the formation of the young Abdullah Mubarak. Indeed, he specifically mentions Abdullah Mubarak's position in the tribal system:

> A woman who suckles two children of opposite sexes, one her own and the other a child of another, makes those children blood brother and sister. They can never marry each other and the boy throughout his life can look upon the face of the girl who nursed with him. They have become foster brother and sister. For example, Abdullah al Mubarak Al-Sabah is foster brother of the daughter of a Rashida woman, the wife of one of the shaikh's *fidawis* [bodyguards], by name Abu Hadida. I know both personally [Abdullah Mubarak and Haya Abu Hadida] and though Abdullah is the son of the late Ruler of Kuwait, he treats the Rashida girl in true foster brother fashion, quite charming to see, and often goes in spring to camp with her father and mother, and is on the friendliest of terms with his foster-sister.[2]

Dickson knew Abdullah Mubarak well, and makes it very clear that he found him 'charming', respectful to his foster parents, and full of brotherly affection for his foster-sister. Brought up in the Bedouin tradition this bore its mark – as Jabbur suggests – throughout his later life, this early cultural influence explaining many of his character traits. As an adult, Abdullah Mubarak was renowned for his generosity. While some city dwellers found this odd, and even an unnecessary extravagance, every Bedouin tribesman would see it quite differently. Dickson explains its significance unequivocally:

> In the piping times of peace, the shaikh must prove himself literally 'the father of his people'. He must know the family troubles of every man and must give good and fair decisions when cases are brought to him for settlement. Above all he must not be miserly, and must keep open house. No name has a more unworthy meaning or leaves a nastier taste in the mouth of the Badawin than the epithet *bakil* or 'stingy one'. Once this name sticks to a chief, his influence is at an end.[3]

Abdullah Mubarak's father had been an exceptional product of a Bedouin warrior culture. Sheikh Mubarak Al-Sabah could take harsh decisions without remorse; he was feared and respected, ruthless in war and in politics. Above all, he had a clarity of vision about the best future for Kuwait. The harshness and rigour of this desert life shaped the behaviour of both men, father and son, in later years. In Abdullah Mubarak's case it was very much like the Jesuit maxim, 'Give us a child before he is seven and he is ours for life'. His character developed during those times spent moving from one grazing ground to another. He learned to be patient, to value generosity in others and to be generous himself. Above all he learned the need for courage, and not to let others deflect him from the path he had chosen. He too could take hard decisions unflinchingly. In the tribal tradition, a leader must have courage, the power of leadership and, most important of all, *hadh* or luck.

What would be his role in life? We know that there was no possibility of Abdullah Mubarak succeeding his father, as in 1921 the Al-Sabah family had chosen his nephew, Sheikh Ahmed al-Jaber, who was much older than the seven-year-old Abdullah Mubarak. Thus it was not Abdullah Mubarak's destiny to be the Ruler of Kuwait. There is no evidence that he ever wished to change this decision, and certainly in later years he never contemplated a struggle for leadership of the state. As a private individual, and with the prestige of being the son of Mubarak Al-Sabah, he had freedom of action such that he could never have enjoyed as the head of state. Yet as the minister who – on behalf of an acquiescent head of state – exercised energetic direct control over the armed forces and public security, and had a portfolio of other responsibilities, he exercised the real day-to-day power.

His inheritance, and his own inclination, was as a modernizer. Participation in so many and varied aspects of Kuwait's public life, for more than two decades, instilled in Abdullah Mubarak a global view of Kuwait's problems and opportunities. He firmly believed that Kuwait's road to progress would be determined by its internal unity, social solidarity and, above all, a commonality of interest between the rulers and the ruled. The ruling family had to speak for the nation and become the crucible of change, looking forwards – not backwards.

§

As the most northerly capital of the Arabian Peninsula, the walled city of Kuwait stood at a key strategic point on the northern shores of the Gulf. The first wall was built in 1760 and protected about 11 hectares. A new wall was built between

1793 and 1811, more substantial than the earlier construction, and extending to 2.3 kilometres. Lorimar described this wall, writing: 'Its thickness is less than one foot; it surrounds the city from the desert side. A trench was dug behind it, with two openings for big guns, each guarding three gates.'

A third wall, built in 1920, was 6.4 kilometres in length, 4.5 metres thick with five main entry gates. By that time, the size of the city state had extended to 72 hectares. None of these walls could have resisted a bombardment, hence the fear of the Ottomans, who had excellent artillery. Yet is faced with Bedouin warriors, equipped only with small arms, or even a Bedouin army, Kuwait could hold them off. The greatest problem would have been lack of water for the people in the city.

The last of these walls was the response to a serious invasion. In early 1920, Ibn Saud had allowed his Ikhwan camel cavalry to push north into Kuwaiti territory, reaching the Red Fort of Jahra, 25 miles from Kuwait city. The Ikhwan were held at Jahra while Sheikh Salem Al-Mubarak, the Ruler, ordered a new defensive wall to be built around the capital. The Kuwaitis erected the new fortification in only 60 days, mobilizing the entire population of Kuwait, and using baked mud and plaster to create a solid and continuous line of defence. As a schoolboy, Abdullah Mubarak was included in the civic guard that manned the walls and gates of the new enceinte, a serious and important role, very rarely given to one so young. His main responsibility was to check the permits of outsiders wanting to pass into the city. By all accounts, he acquired the reputation for being firm, honest and not permitting any violation of the regulations that he had been told to enforce.

Until the 1940s, Kuwait was little more than a small city state. The wall around Kuwait was a symbol of the city's security, still with a military value but by the twentieth century equally an emblem of the city's status. There were not many walled cities in Arabia. The wall was pierced by five well-defended city gates; inside the walls, little had changed over the centuries. The houses were made of clay or rock from the sea, the streets narrow and unpaved. A municipal government had been set up in 1930 and a municipal council elected two years later. The surrounding wall was only removed in the remodelling of the city in the late 1950s and 1960s,[4] when Abdullah Mubarak was at the height of his powers. It meant carrying through the first plan for a new Kuwait completed in 1951 by a firm of British architects: Minoprio, Spencely and McFarlane.

Minoprio later wrote: 'It was a difficult commission. We didn't know anything much about the Muslim world and the Kuwaitis wanted a city – they wanted a new city, hospitals, schools, housing and good communications. All that we could give them was what we knew.' Their main objective had been to set up the guidelines for future development. They focused on a new road and street network, sites for new public buildings, housing, parks and sports grounds. However, the core of their plan revolved around the need to create 'a beautiful and dignified town centre', befitting what was by then a major supplier of the world's oil. The Ruler headed the Kuwait Development Board, established in 1950, but Abdullah Mubarak frequently deputized for him, often for long periods. The development of a new city was a priority, for all the reasons given by Minoprio. For Abdullah Mubarak, only a new city could symbolize the determination to achieve change – and he was always a force for promoting change.

At that time there was no official census detailing how many people lived in Kuwait city, and estimates of the population varied wildly. Sheikh Hafez Wahba, an Egyptian who lived in Kuwait city for some years and then worked for King Abdul Aziz Al-Saud, becoming Saudi Arabia's Ambassador to the United Kingdom in the 1960s, estimated the number at 15,000.[5] In 1908, Lorimer had estimated the population of the whole of Kuwait as about 35,000, mostly drawn from the Arab tribes of Otobees, Awazem, Bani Khaled, Rashaida, Ojman, Dawaser, Al-Aniza, Dhafer and the Arabs from Ihsa'a and Baharneh.

§

There are also tantalizingly few references to Abdullah Mubarak's life between 1926 and 1940. We know that several members of the family recognized his talents from an early age. One was Sheikh Hamad Mubarak Al-Sabah, his elder brother, who took good care of him and saw that he came to no harm. Sheikh Ahmed al-Jaber, his nephew who ruled Kuwait during the period 1921–50, entrusted Abdullah Mubarak with a range of important responsibilities, including the post of deputy director of the Security Department. His superior in the department, Sheikh Ali al-Khalifa al-Abdullah Al-Sabah, the director, regarded him with considerable respect. Sheikh Ali was one of Kuwait's most successful military leaders who fought bravely in the Al Jahra battle of 1920.[6] He was Abdullah Mubarak's mentor and guide in all aspects of Kuwait's national security, helping him to understand the many threats and the ways of dealing with them. British documents begin to note his role from the early 1940s, but only in passing. It was when the Ruler selected him as deputy director of the Security Department that his distinguished career in public service began. Of course, being the son of Mubarak the Great certainly helped his steady rise, but the key factor was nevertheless his reputation for fulfilling his duties faithfully and reliably.

We know that Abdullah Mubarak began his education in the city after spending his early life in the desert. He attended a small religious school before joining the main Mubarakiya School, founded in 1911 and named after his father. Even as a schoolboy he took his role as the son of Sheikh Mubarak Al-Sabah extremely seriously and, to those around him, made a point of displaying a strong sense of duty and personal responsibility. He first took part in public life as an assistant to Sheikh Ali al-Khalifa al-Abdullah Al-Sabah, the governor of Kuwait city and the director of its Security Department. In the 1930s, Abdullah Mubarak was responsible for fighting smuggling, which was increasing exponentially at that time due to Kuwait's position on the coast and its openness on the landward side, with extensive smuggling in foodstuffs, other goods and stolen livestock flourishing between Kuwait and Iraq.

Smuggling created problems and tension among the tribes and between Iraq and Kuwait. During the 1930s the Iraqi Government adopted strict measures on land and maritime trade, tightening supervision on the flow of goods. One consequence was an interruption to the city's vital water supply, carried by ships from Shatt Al-Arab to Kuwait. This was a serious matter. The British Political Agent, Colonel Dickson, visited the border area and discussed the difficulties with the chiefs of the Iraqi and Kuwaiti tribes so as to reach a speedy solution. The water supply was restored, and Abdullah Mubarak was put in charge of combatting the smugglers. At that time the government institutions, systems and departments necessary for effective action simply did not exist. The Kuwait Government did not even have its own vehicles, so Abdullah Mubarak had no alternative but to hire taxicabs and lorries to chase the smugglers. During these hectic pursuits, which today seem almost comical, many dangerous confrontations occurred with smugglers. Yet there was nothing at all comical about the potential violence of these encounters, with Abdullah Mubarak facing death more than once as he regularly confronted smugglers armed with guns and swords who had no inhibitions about using them.

This was an unrelenting campaign. Abdullah Mubarak and his team worked deep in the desert under conditions of extreme hardship. On patrol or in strikes against groups of smugglers, he and his men slept on the sand with only the desert brushwood as their pillows, their head cloths becoming face masks against the dust and blown sand. They drank the same water as the sheep and camels and, in the intense summer heat, cooled themselves by jumping into the oases, afterwards drying their clothes in the hot desert breeze while they slept.

His childhood initiation into desert life proved invaluable. It was essential to establish close relations with the tribes and their sheikhs in Kuwait and Saudi Arabia, especially the sheikhs of Ojman, Mutran, Shummer, Aniza, Muntafeq, Roula, Huweitat, Sukhur, Shararat, Rashaida and Awazem. Fostering tribal loyalty gave him enormous political leverage, but it grew out of a mutual respect. He took the time to honour these tribal leaders, sitting and talking with them, fulfilling the demands of Arab courtesy. He may have been the son of Sheikh Mubarak, the redoubtable late Ruler of Kuwait, but he quickly recognized that as a young man it was essential for him to show respect to the tribal leaders. The series of relationships that developed gave him a unique understanding of the true problems facing the people. In consequence, after a very short time, he was able to restore political and social stability in the desert and along the coast.

There was one incident in 1940 that displayed the steel in his personality. Two servants of Princess Noura, the sister of King

Abdul Aziz Al-Saud of Saudi Arabia, attacked some Kuwaitis in Kuwait. When the victims complained to Abdullah Mubarak, he punished the two Saudis in accordance with Kuwaiti law. When King Abdul Aziz heard of their punishment, he was furious and felt humiliated. He immediately demanded the extradition of those who were responsible for beating his sister's servants. The normal practice would have been to send a few scapegoats to Riyadh, where they would be summarily executed. Yet some members of the Al-Sabah family thought Abdullah Mubarak should take responsibility and submit himself to the King. This would avoid any action against Kuwait by its powerful neighbour, whom the Kuwaitis dared not risk provoking. Young Abdullah had little choice. He bade farewell to his mother, who believed she would never see him again, and left for Saudi Arabia accompanied by his superior at the Public Security Department, Sheikh Ali Al-Khalifa.[7]

When they arrived in Riyadh they went immediately to Abdul Aziz's *majlis*. Abdullah Mubarak greeted the King and took a seat some distance from the Ruler, which was a sign of courtesy on account of his youth, while Sheikh Ali Al-Khalifa sat closer to the King, who immediately asked the younger man to give an account of what had happened. Abdullah Mubarak spoke quietly but confidently. He said that the Saudi servants had not respected Kuwaiti traditions and, therefore, he had punished them; had any Kuwaiti misbehaved in Saudi Arabia, the King would undoubtedly have punished him, as guests should observe the traditions of the host country. The King questioned him for some time and then, to the surprise of those attending the *majlis*, asked Abdullah Mubarak to sit beside him: 'You did the right thing. Had you not been confident of this, you would not have come here. You are the son of our dear friend [Mubarak Al-Sabah] who did so much for us.'

With these words King Abdul Aziz came to the heart of the matter: he owed his life to Sheikh Mubarak. The future King Abdul Aziz had attempted to seize power in the Saudi capital, Riyadh, and failed. In danger of instant execution, he evaded his enemies and took refuge in Kuwait between 1893 and 1902. There Sheikh Mubarak treated him with respect and gave him back his dignity after his ignominious flight. Abdul Aziz's successful campaign to capture Riyadh had begun in Kuwait, where Abdullah Mubarak's father had given him sanctuary and refused to yield him to his enemies, at considerable risk to Kuwait's political interests. This personal bond, a debt of honour, was unbreakable. How far Abdullah Mubarak had anticipated the outcome, given the circumstances, is impossible to say. But he either made the right decision or showed considerable boldness. The King asked Abdullah Mubarak to stay on as his guest; when he finally left for home the King gave him many presents, including two Ford cars, one of which Abdullah Mubarak had in his possession until the Iraqi invasion in 1990, when the occupation forces destroyed his family home.

When Sheikh Ali Al-Khalifa died in 1942, Abdullah Mubarak succeeded him as Chief of the Public Security Department and as Governor of Kuwait City. Thanks to Emir Sheikh Ahmed al Jaber's encouragement and patronage, Abdullah Mubarak's responsibilities grew steadily, especially during the years of World War II. In appreciation of his efforts, in 1945 the British Government awarded him the Companion of the Most Eminent Order of the Indian Empire (CIE) for the contribution he had made to good government in Kuwait. There was another reason for their gratitude: he had not opposed the British position when the government of Iraq was overturned by a *coup d'état* led by Prime Minister Rashid Ali in April 1941. On 17 April, Rashid Ali had asked Germany to support his government against any British intervention, which triggered an immediate military response from the British Government. The British Army took control of Iraq in May 1941, when it seemed likely that Prime Minister Rashid Ali had called in German and Italian forces. In fact, a Luftwaffe squadron was indeed based at a former RAF airfield inside Iraq and temporarily dominated Iraqi airspace. In that situation, with the British Army heavily outnumbered, it was essential that troops from Britain's Indian Army should be able to land in Kuwait if they could not land in Basra. It was entirely possible that the Iraqi Army would oppose a landing at Basra port. The message received by the British (and we may assume it came from Abdullah Mubarak's office) was that in the case of an emergency, Kuwait's port would not be blocked.[8]

Following the award of the CIE, it seems all the more extraordinary that, in the years after 1946, a few British political officers in Kuwait regarded Abdullah Mubarak with deep suspicion, and even as a danger to the smooth running of the state. This change coincided with Kuwait's new status as an increasingly important oil producer. Abdullah Mubarak's increasingly significant role in the government and administration, and his confidence in challenging British policy when he felt it was not in the interests of his country, made him a marked man.

Abdullah Mubarak's rise continued, as his responsibilities and duties grew. His pre-eminence was recognized in 1958 when the Emir, Sheikh Abdullah Al-Salem, authorized a Higher Council formed of the 17 department heads, with Sheikh Abdullah Mubarak second in the list, immediately after the Emir himself. The decree defined his responsibilities as 'Chief of the Public Security Department, supervising the Nationality and Passports Administration, Radio and T.V. and some other duties'. He was followed in rank by Sheikh Abdullah al-Ahmed al-Jaber Al-Sabah, head of the defence force attached to public security; Sheikh Abdullah al-Jaber Al-Sabah, head of education, courts and *awqaf* departments; Sheikh Fahad al-Salem Al-Sabah, head of public works, health and the municipality departments; and Sheikh Sabah al-Salem Al-Sabah, as chief of police.

The council was a significant step forward in terms of Kuwait's institution-building. It ratified laws, endorsed regulations and approved the budget. In the following year the Emir merged the Police and Public Security into one department under Sheikh Abdullah Mubarak.

Perhaps the best measure of his position comes from the regional press. Fekri Abaza, an eminent Egyptian intellectual, was from 1924 the outspoken editor-in-chief of the Cairo newspaper *Al Muzawwar*. He wrote of Abdullah Mubarak in 1958, saying that he was very far from the dry official or bureaucrat and that he would be 'a hard act to follow'.[9] In return, Abdullah Mubarak made it clear that Egyptians should feel completely at home in Kuwait, stating: 'When the small Kuwaiti state was in its youth it obtained every educational, political and technical support from Egypt' and 'this cannot be forgotten'. Even the British authorities, often suspicious of Abdullah Mubarak's political attitudes and Arab nationalist loyalties, gave further measure of his position when, as early as 1951, they described him as a 'proud and dignified man'.[10] However, this was not necessarily a compliment; in official parlance it could also suggest that he was a problem, sometimes 'a thorn in the flesh' of those who had to impose the British Government's wishes on Kuwait.

Some of the comments were deliberately fulsome. In 1951, an Arab writer judged that the Sheikh 'possessed all the qualities of a prudent ruler' and that 'he was always fair and unbiased' in his decisions.[11] Fadel Saeed Aql recorded the remarks of the Lebanese press delegation that visited Kuwait in March 1952,[12] who found Abdullah Mubarak charming, confident, sharp, eloquent, and with a profound love for his people.[13] However, Abdullah Mubarak scorned egregious flattery, and was genuinely more interested in the opinion of Kuwait's citizens. Senior Kuwaiti citizens still remember the open window of his office overlooking the street at the Public Security Department. Every citizen or foreign resident could speak to the Sheikh in person about any problem or with any request, in accordance with the old Arab custom. He related easily to ordinary people and understood their needs and aspirations. This was confirmed in a report prepared by an official of the British Foreign Office, escorting Abdullah Mubarak during one of his visits to Britain. He reported that when he once visited the Sheikh, he found him sitting on the floor and playing cards with his servants. Yet what the British admired most about him was how hard he worked. Many Kuwaiti officials adopted a very short working day, arriving late and leaving early. This was not how Abdullah Mubarak operated, whose work was a pleasure to him. The Political Agent noted in 1959 that 'the Sheikh begins his day at 6:30 a.m. and works until midnight, and apart from two hours rest after lunch, he works all day'.[14]

Abdullah Mubarak was a modernizer within a traditional society and, unlike many other modernizers in the Arab lands, he had the social status and the political authority to put his plans into action. None of his ideas were particularly radical; in his early adult years he became an ardent believer in the power of science and education, convinced that a brighter future for Kuwait could only come through education. Well-equipped schools were a prominent feature of the new Kuwait.

More than merely a good administrator, he showed a passionate dedication in every aspect of his work. Higher education was one of his passions. He travelled widely and, in all his foreign visits, made time to meet Kuwaiti students studying abroad, no matter how tight his schedule. At first there were not many Kuwaiti students abroad, and he recognized the problems caused by their isolation. At these meetings he exhorted them to work hard and to be a credit to their country, whilst also encouraging them to divulge any obstacles to success placed in their paths. He might then intervene with the academic authorities on their behalf, or provide more money where it was needed for books and other educational materials. These students studying overseas were the future pioneers who would fight to establish, develop and sustain a modern Kuwait. They had great opportunities as a result of their education and he had the conviction to support them for the future. When they returned to Kuwait he wrote letters of recommendation, or sometimes directed his colleagues in government departments to secure suitable employment for them.

Another significant characteristic of Sheikh Abdullah Mubarak was his instinctive religious tolerance. During an interview for *Al-Musawer* magazine, regarding the construction of a church in Kuwait, he said that while Kuwaitis were Muslims, nonetheless: 'We are building a church because foreign and Arab Christians in Kuwait have the right to perform their religious rites. Our objective is to make all in Kuwait comfortable and happy.'[15] Moreover, he made it a practice to visit Christians working in Kuwait during their holy days and religious festivities. His private physician, Eid Shammas, was a Christian and it was widely known that Abdullah Mubarak trusted him implicitly with all matters concerning his health. He also sought Shammas's advice on medical policy for Kuwait.

Religious tolerance was fundamental to all his actions and conduct. He felt deeply honoured when the Orthodox Patriarch of Antioch, in communion with Rome, awarded him the rare distinction of the Grand Order of St Marcus in 1960. Like the award of the CIE by the British Government in 1945, he believed that it was an honour to Kuwait as well as to him personally. The new Pope, Paul VI, invited him to visit the Vatican, an invitation that Abdullah Mubarak happily accepted, making his visit in December 1963.

Many people remember most his generous spirit. In *Forty Years in Kuwait*, Violet Dickson (the wife of H. R. P. Dickson) recalls that by the end of February 1943 the number of pilgrims passing through Kuwait en route to Mecca had exceeded 8,000. This made finding transport for all of them very difficult. A few pilgrims arrived late after the main body had departed and they became Abdullah Mubarak's guests. There were no cars or trucks available, so he contacted Colonel Dickson, Violet's husband, asking to borrow or to buy his car. When Dickson hesitated, the Sheikh gave him a cheque for 45,000 rupees, which was far in excess of the vehicle's value. The Sheikh then gave the car to the pilgrims for their journey to the Holy City, ex gratia. When they made the return journey through Kuwait, they again became his guests.[16]

The evidence of all these stories is that Abdullah Mubarak had the rare gift of making people feel at ease. He had strong opinions and was known to be headstrong, but he never let this get in the way of human contact. The British officials in Kuwait expressed their political disquiet in their reports of his speeches, their analysis of his policies and in describing his powerful rhetoric. Yet he was the Kuwaiti they were always most pleased to see, a man with great charm, who could nonetheless argue his case relentlessly, with verve and aplomb. At the same time, they knew that they would soon have to write a critical report about him to the Political Resident in Bahrain, suggesting that he might be a danger to British interests.

This tone of negative comment was the style of official writing instilled in all those who served in the Gulf. They were trained to see it as their duty to inform their superiors fully and dispassionately as to any threat or danger to British interests and policy. They were discouraged from becoming too involved in the internal affairs of their territory or from expressing their own preferences, except in the most guarded terms. While a new policy was being formulated they were encouraged to express and justify their own opinions, but once a policy had been agreed, all critical discussion had to end.

In Kuwait the policy stakes were higher than in most of the other Gulf postings, first because of its oil output, and second because of its strategic position at the head of the Gulf and between Saudi Arabia and Iraq. Kuwait's oil production totalled 5.9 million barrels in 1946, 16.2 million barrels in 1947, and then continued to rise steadily until 1972. The British Government was keen that British Petroleum should continue to dominate Kuwait's oil concessions through the Kuwait Oil Company. However, Kuwait preferred to broaden its customer base, signing agreements for new fields with Aminoil (a consortium of US companies) in 1948, with production beginning in 1953, and with the Arabian Oil Company (owned by Japanese interests) in 1958. Kuwait also wanted to develop a refinery and downstream activity, setting up the Kuwait National Petroleum Company in 1960. All these developments took place while Abdullah Mubarak occupied the seat of power in Kuwait, and all of them worked directly against the British perception of the United Kingdom's national interest.

—2—

State-Building in Kuwait: The Role of Abdullah Mubarak

Most observers of Kuwait's modern history and of Sheikh Abdullah Mubarak's role within it regard his greatest contribution as developing the machinery of government – building the institutions that forged the modern state of Kuwait. Institution-building is the process of creating governmental and non-governmental structures, introducing procedures and codes of conduct in a society; it represents the evolution from haphazard governance to governance underpinned by laws and procedures – and is fundamental to modernization, and economic and social change.

Institution-building is at the heart of political development. Abdullah Mubarak had an understanding of the role of institutions in a modern state. He also had a native intuition that the essence of progress in Kuwait would be flexibility in implementing change. Having neither a blueprint of the reforms he wanted to introduce, nor any fixed timetable, he regarded all these as pragmatic political decisions. Nevertheless, his objective was consistent and he explained it very clearly. Power and authority would remain as before, with the Emir at the centre of the nation. However, Kuwait needed a new framework of government fully capable of running a modern state. In some cases, this would require the creation of new departments covering important matters such as strategy and planning – essential in a country where its oil revenues were spiralling upwards. On other matters, such as national defence, it made more sense to merge existing ministries, preserving the best of the past while ensuring the armed forces as a whole were more combat-ready and better equipped.

From the outset, Abdullah Mubarak knew that reliable progress would only develop by bringing together a number of separate and distinct strands. The prime example was civil aviation, in which he was one of the pioneers for the Middle East. He regarded it as one of the transforming influences in the postwar world; any Middle East country that did not have good connections to Europe and the United States, as well as to all the neighbouring countries, was ultimately doomed to decline. However, this was problematic because aviation was one of the more jealously guarded areas of British control. To achieve the development of aviation he thus had to adopt an indirect approach, avoiding head-on conflict with the British Government, which did not favour Kuwait making this kind of progress.

Within aviation there was a separate but closely connected strand of military aviation. Of concern to Kuwait was that its powerful neighbours had military aircraft while Kuwait did not. The nation had no possibility of defending itself against attack from the air. While acquiring an air force at first posed a political problem with the British, in the end there were few objections if the valuable contract for the warplanes went to a British company, followed by other lucrative contracts with Britain for maintenance and training. In the end, the British Government felt that economic advantage might outweigh political and strategic principle; it changed its policy and supplied the planes. Once Kuwait had its own national airline, founded in 1954, air links with the whole world, and its own military fighter planes protecting the nation's air space, Abdullah Mubarak knew that Kuwait had the attributes of a modern state. Although a small state like Kuwait could not hope to overcome larger states, the possession of an effective defence force would act as a deterrent to any threat of invasion.

Abdullah Mubarak had an easier task with his other reforms. He instigated the building of Al-Ahmadi port in 1951, which proved so successful that a major expansion was ordered in 1957.[1] He set up the Department of Labour, Statistics and Immigration and pushed through a Chamber of Commerce and Industry. In his capacity as head of the Council of Education, he supervised the tremendous expansion of education to prepare a new generation of qualified Kuwaitis capable of operating the new economy. He supported the expanding role of private business and was sympathetic to the aspirations of Kuwaiti entrepreneurs. He was instrumental in the opening of the Al-Ahli Club, the first forum where educated Kuwaitis could meet and talk to their peers, and became its honorary chair. Establishing the club was the first stage in developing the social institutions of civil society.

His consistent attitude was that all these changes were not for the benefit of his generation but for younger Kuwaitis; the 20- and 30-year-olds would, in a few years' time, be the managers and officials of the new Kuwait. Once both internal and external security had been established, the machinery of government built and possession taken of Kuwait's oil resources, Abdullah Mubarak knew that his country would be the model small state for the Arab world.

Providing safety and security

The most significant institutions in most developing states are those that provide security and stability, both internally and in preventing threats from neighbouring states. Abdullah Mubarak was the key actor in both areas. He first built up the institutions of public security and safety within Kuwait, and second, recognized the need for an army and air force to protect Kuwait from external threats.

The Public Security Department opened on 12 December 1939, when Sheikh Ahmed al-Jaber, the Emir of Kuwait, resolved to establish an organization for maintaining security and managing contact with the tribes. The department was located at Safat Square in the downtown area of Kuwait. The first paved street in the city, completed in 1945, was Dasman Street that ran from Dasman Palace (the Emir's residence) to Safat Square near to the newly established Public Security Department. The head of the department was Sheikh Ali-al-Khalifa Al-Sabah, with Abdullah Mubarak as his right-hand man. In April 1942, Sheikh Ali died and Sheikh Abdullah Mubarak, who was by then 28 years old, took his place at the head of the department. The son of the Emir, Sheikh Abdullah al-Ahmed al-Jaber Al-Sabah, was his deputy until his premature death in January 1957.[2]

The department had a modest beginning. In 1942, it had only three employees: Abdul-Latif Faisal Al-Thuwaini, Othman Bu Qammaz and Amin Singer. In 1948, Abdullah Mubarak founded the first Public Security Training School and donated the land on which it was built. He appointed Mohammed Abu Kuhail as its first head. In 1948, the Emir asked Abdullah Mubarak to establish a department for passports and travel, which officially opened on 1 January 1949. Travel in and out of Kuwait was growing, and the old system was slow and inefficient. He appointed Hani Qaddoumi, a Palestinian, as his assistant. The passport department was at Safat Square, and the Emir attended the opening ceremony. Perhaps another reason for creating the passport office was as a challenge to the British Government, which claimed authority to control all travel in and out of Kuwait, on the grounds that Kuwait did not have the capacity to carry out the necessary work.

By 1950, Abdullah Mubarak had seen the need to expand the Public Security Department, bringing in well-qualified security and police experts. He turned down a proposal to take on some NCOs from the British military police. Ever the Arab nationalist he preferred to recruit Palestinian officers who had served in the Palestine police under the British mandate. He also selected other police officers from Syria and Lebanon.[3] With this team of experienced officers to carry out his orders, and to oversee the lower ranks, Abdullah Mubarak managed the public security service with great skill and competence; later, he spoke proudly of how safe Kuwait had become and how theft was a rare crime.[4] It was his first major success.

A Syrian commentator succinctly described public security in Kuwait: 'Kuwaiti prisons are empty: Security prevails in Kuwait, thanks to the efforts of Sheikh Abdullah Mubarak, chief of Public Security. I have neither seen nor heard of any conflicts among the indigenous Kuwaitis. The prison there contained only 67 prisoners in 1952: 9 Kuwaitis and 58 foreigners. They were imprisoned for minor infractions and some more serious matters – default on debts or traffic accidents. Thefts in Kuwait were rare, indeed almost non-existent.'[5]

Abdullah Mubarak made the nation's internal security the centre point of his administration. The British author John Daniels states that Abdullah Mubarak ran his department with a firm hand and expected the highest standards from those who wore a police uniform.[6] As head of the department he often reiterated: 'The Police and Public Security must constantly watch over the homeland's security and national interests. They will monitor the steps of anyone who thinks of violating security and order in the country. We will not hesitate to confront such cases with all necessary firmness and strictness.'[7] If we take into account the extent of social change in Kuwait during the 1950s, the influx of tens of thousands of foreign labourers and the unstable regional conditions, his firmness and dogged resolution were an absolute necessity. In the early 1950s, a detailed official report by the Political Agent into the organization of the Public Security Department gave a very positive assessment of what had been achieved.[8] The report said that Sheikh Abdullah Mubarak directed the department wisely and personally supervised every detail. The forces of the department were divided into two main groups: one for border protection, that is the area beyond the wall; the other for safeguarding security in the city area inside the wall. The 'border defence force' was at that time Kuwait's only military unit, and not a police unit at all. The creation of a Kuwait army was a major step that took place in 1953. However, even after 1955, the roles of internal security and border defence remained entirely distinct.

Sheikh Abdullah Mubarak's work in the Public Security Department allowed him to gain deep insight into the tensions in Kuwaiti society and politics. Always an impatient man, his style was characterized by rapid action and a decisive manner.

As his experience increased, his confidence grew and he was better able to face the increasingly challenging world around him.

The growing instability of the Arab world caused much concern in Kuwait. The early 1950s witnessed the outbreak of the revolution in Egypt, the British commitment to withdraw from its Suez base – the largest in the region – and the conflict between Cairo and Baghdad (1955), after the establishment of the Baghdad Pact that included Iraq, Pakistan, Iran and Britain.

In 1956 there was a major confrontation between Egypt and the main Western powers. When the World Bank and the US withdrew their offer to finance the construction of the Aswan High Dam, President Gamal Abdul Nasser retaliated by nationalizing the Suez Canal Company. This was followed by the tripartite attack (Britain, France and Israel) against Egypt, which ignited pan-Arab fury. It was only the US recognition that its own interests were jeopardized by this rash action that impelled President Eisenhower to use America's financial muscle to force a British and French withdrawal. This prevented Arab indignation from boiling over.

In 1957, the United States proposed a scheme known as the 'Eisenhower Plan' to fill the so-called 'vacuum' in the Middle East. This was supported by the governments of Jordan, Lebanon and Iraq. However, the polarization between revolutionary and conservative regimes in the Arab region was becoming more acute. On 28 February 1958, Egypt and Syria amazed the whole world when they united in a single state, which was to be called the United Arab Republic (UAR). The response from the conservative pro-Western states was rapid. The Hashemite Union between Jordan and Iraq (both ruled by Hashemite monarchs) was announced in May as a counterbalance to the UAR.

Yet this union proved short-lived; in July 1958, revolution broke out in Iraq, sweeping away the Hashemite monarchy. The transfer of power was brutal – King Faisal II, his uncle Prince 'Abd al-Ilah the former regent, and most of the royal family were machine-gunned in the palace courtyard; Prime Minister Nouri As-Sa'eed was caught while trying to escape from the city in disguise. He was shot and his body dragged through the streets and severely mutilated. The new regime terminated the union with Jordan, pulled Iraq out of the Baghdad Pact and moved closer to Egypt. However, once settled in power, the leader of the Iraqi coup, Brigadier Abdul Karim Qassem, by then Iraq's undisputed new ruler, allied himself closely to the local communists and the Soviet Union. At the same time, President Nasser, increasingly suspicious of the Soviet Union, began purging the Egyptian communists; Iraq's rapprochement with Cairo ended and a new stage of inter-Arab conflict began.

Kuwait was not impervious to all the changes sweeping through the Arab world. Arab opinion was becoming more outspoken in its challenge to British influence in the Gulf. For the first time, the questions aired only in private by Abdullah Mubarak were coming out into the open, challenging the British oil companies' controlling interests in the area. US political and diplomatic pressure was steadily applied to Britain in the aftermath of the Suez failure, while radicals encouraged by Nasser and Qassem began to take more direct action. Sixteen bombs exploded in the Kuwaiti oilfields, aimed at the pumping facilities, while a number of other time bombs were detected before detonation.

The position of the Kuwaiti Government and of Abdullah Mubarak was both delicate and precarious. On the one hand, it was impossible to adopt a neutral approach or even to ignore the Arab nationalist sentiments, increasingly popular among

Kuwaitis. Besides, Abdullah Mubarak had strong private sympathies with Egypt's decision to nationalize the Suez Canal Company. On the other hand, the British authorities in Kuwait still dominated the country, claiming the right to steer its foreign policy and to oversee foreign access. In London, the menace of pan-Arab nationalism was a particular *bête noire* of the Foreign Office, which put relentless pressure on the British officials in Kuwait. Abdullah Mubarak's response to this tricky situation in the autumn of 1956 was an attempt to be both adroit and nuanced at the same time, a high-wire act that was only partially successful.

To cool the rising passions of ordinary Kuwaitis Abdullah Mubarak sought to defuse the tension, while at the same time raising the strength and readiness of the security forces. He first met the leaders of the Arab nationalist groups and told them that supporting Egypt would not be achieved by destroying pipelines or throwing bombs, but by providing money for Egypt's defence: 'For those who want to donate funds, the door is open. I must tell you I am the first donor. For those who want to fight (alongside Egypt), planes and arms are available in Egypt for you. I will personally guarantee your transportation to Egypt if that is what you truly want.' This speech was characteristic of his approach through the following months. Many in his audience were young men for whom he had been an advisor and, in some cases, a patron. 'I am with you in spirit,' he said, 'but what is the best way in which we can support the cause?' It was very much *we*. He promised to be 'the first donor' and, in almost every case, he successfully turned them away from the course of direct action and violence. Abdullah Mubarak neatly defused the crisis and 'saved the day' as Ralph Hewins has expressed it. His was a pragmatic answer to the problem confronting the leaders of Kuwait.[9]

Later, however, his warm words entrapped him. Repeated in the reports to London, shorn of their context, they made him sound like a rabble-rouser. In fact, the reverse was true. It is quite correct that he was a passionate Arab nationalist, but his head controlled his heart, and he understood the real danger that lay hidden in the turmoil. The bullet-ridden corpses in Baghdad had been a terrifying warning to those in authority in every Gulf state.

The first report of the Political Agent to London on 1 November 1956 was measured and fair to Abdullah Mubarak: 'He immediately took control of the highly volatile situation. He talked to the social and sports clubs' representatives and told them that if order was not maintained, British forces would occupy Kuwait, as had happened in Bahrain, and that would represent a major setback to Kuwait's political development.'[10]

As the head of security, Abdullah Mubarak refused point-blank to grant permission for any demonstrations. He recognized that the British were waiting for any excuse to intervene in the country. So when the public gathered en masse at the Souk Mosque, Abdullah Mubarak persuaded Sheikh Sa'ad Al-Abdulla (later Crown Prince of Kuwait) and Sheikh Abdulla Al-Jaber to go there and tell the protestors of 'the presence of a British Fleet off our coasts' and to ask them to remain orderly and to disperse. Under no circumstances should they provide the British with any excuse to intervene.[11] On 2 November, the police force was placed under Abdullah Mubarak's direct command, and thereafter public security forces and the police jointly patrolled the streets, resulting in a skilful management of the crisis that served to increase considerably his influence and prestige.[12]

The growing public demand for pan-Arabism grew out of the Egyptian refusal to submit to pressure from the Western governments. Egypt's resistance, the blocking of the Suez Canal and the humiliation of Britain and France had produced a powerful movement against the exercise of 'colonial' power in Arab lands. Kuwait, where political apathy had been the norm, had been transformed into a state where the people would come out onto the street and protest angrily.

One new element of instability was that by the mid-1950s Kuwait was no longer the simple unitary society it had been in earlier decades. Like any Gulf oil state, its population had been swollen by a massive influx from outside, both Arabs and non-Arabs. As a result, with this complex and volatile social mix, how the population would respond to the tumultuous events of 1956 was now difficult to gauge. Certainly, by 1957 Kuwait was witnessing increasing activity by revolutionary and leftist elements inside the established social clubs, but also more widely among the new population. Leaflets appeared on the street demanding demonstrations, and celebration of the socialist May Day holiday.

In response, Abdullah Mubarak met some of the most prominent Kuwaiti personalities and warned that demonstrations were banned because they would harm Kuwait's interests and stability, and that any demonstration would be promptly suppressed. With the police and public order forces ever-present on the streets, it was clear that he meant what he said. According to US documents, Abdullah Mubarak said: 'There will be no demonstrations in Kuwait … Assemblies, speeches … Yes. But no demonstrations.'[13] The threat worked and there were no demonstrations. Most important, he signalled to Washington and to London that Kuwait would continue to be a reliable ally.

Another political crisis emerged at the beginning of February 1959 on the first anniversary of Egyptian–Syrian unity. It all began calmly with Abdullah Mubarak (then acting as Deputy Ruler) giving an address on the state radio applauding this example of Arab unity, and declaring that the next day would be a public holiday commemorating the occasion.[14] This not only reflected Abdullah Mubarak's underlying beliefs but also avoided public disturbance, because the state had taken a lead. The popular reaction seemed largely positive. The next day all government departments were duly closed for the public holiday and crowds gathered in front of the Public Security Department to cheer Sheikh Abdullah Mubarak. He appeared and gave another speech about the importance and necessity of Arab unity.

So far everything had remained peaceful. However, after Abdullah Mubarak's speech, the sports and social clubs felt emboldened. They called for an open public meeting at Shuwaikh School. Abdullah Mubarak, perhaps over-confident, permitted the meeting to take place but upon strict conditions. He insisted that the meeting should not arouse the crowd and that the organizers would be held personally responsible for any demonstrations. His reasoning was that demonstrations gave agitators and communists an opening to divert the gathering from its objective. This would then provide the British with an excuse to intervene in Kuwait's internal affairs.

The meeting was on an unprecedented scale. According to the Political Agent's estimate, about 20,000 persons – a vast gathering from almost every social group – assembled around the school. Well-educated young men, often members of the elite social and sports clubs, rubbed shoulders with local working men and foreign workers in the oil industry. The meeting began at about 2.30 p.m. with the first speech by Dr Ahmed Al-Khatib, who gave a sober statement on Arab unity. Next to speak, however, was Jassem Al-Qatami who took a very different line. He railed against Abdullah Mubarak, the Al-Sabah family and the entire political system in Kuwait. By the time the next speaker, the famous radio presenter Ahmad Sa'id from the Voice of the Arabs Radio, came to the microphone the crowd was in a dangerous mood. He tried to defuse the tension with a moving and impassioned speech about every Arab's birthright, Arab unity.

However, the inflammatory force of Al-Qatami's heady rhetoric had transformed the crowd into an angry mob. He had deliberately abandoned the agreed theme of the meeting – Arab unity – and for the first time directly challenged the power and legitimacy of the Kuwaiti political system. The situation had become all the more dangerous because the meeting was held with the sanction of the government. The presence at the meeting of Sheikh Abdullah Al-Jaber, head of the Education Department, gave the unfortunate (and inaccurate) impression that some senior members of the government might even support Al-Qatami's line. The police who were shadowing the meeting from a distance followed Abdullah Mubarak's orders. They closed in, fired warning shots and then aimed at the crowd. Serious clashes broke out immediately. The meeting was finally dispersed when the security forces, strongly reinforced, broke up the demonstration.

Abdullah Mubarak responded immediately with a complete crackdown on dissent. He issued an edict banning all the leading clubs: namely, the Graduates Club, the National Cultural Club, the Teachers' Club and the Arab Union Club. Newspapers such as *Al-Fajr* and *Al-Sha'ab*, which were held to have encouraged the outburst, were closed down and certain named individuals were banned from travelling abroad.

Although at first sight it might seem that this resolute action would have strengthened his personal position, in fact it did the reverse. He was blamed, for different reasons, by many disparate groups. He was criticized for allowing the meeting in the first place, blamed for allowing it to get out of hand, and then denounced for the use of force with which it was ended. In retrospect, the central problem was that one of the speakers – Al-Qatami – broke the agreement as to the tone and content of the meeting. All the other speakers abided by the conditions under which the meeting was permitted.

Abdullah Mubarak, by stationing police close to the school, had covered the risk of the huge meeting turning into a demonstration. There was no wider disorder spreading through the city. However, he may have made a misjudgement. He saw the source of the problem primarily in the clubs and associations, which he knew well, where the affluent and educated Kuwaitis congregated. He was not fully aware of the greater threat posed by the mass of angry working men and foreign workers who had also joined the meeting. The anonymous mass of non-Kuwaitis outside the constraints and norms of Kuwaiti society posed a different challenge: the mob was unlike any earlier gathering, both in scale and composition. It was impossible to manage. He would not make the same mistake again.

Most writers attributed this crisis to Abdullah Mubarak's penchant for Arab nationalism, which they felt had prevented him from fulfilling his official position as head of the Public Security Department, responsible for implementing the Supreme Council's decisions. This was entirely untrue. In fact, the real difficulty grew from the changing policy attitude in Washington. The US Government had been wrong-footed by the British, French and Israeli attack on Egypt, and responded by forcing a ceasefire. Thereafter, the US had recalibrated its Middle East policy in simplistic terms. What was happening in the region was the opening of a new front in the global Cold War. The agent of disruption was Gamal Abdul Nasser, who was the instrument of Soviet objectives. He (as the British had clearly stated) had to be stopped. 'Nasserism' entered the US political vocabulary as a synecdoche for godless communism.

This shift was clearly evident in US reports of the disturbances in Kuwait. They referred to Abdullah Mubarak's warm feeling for Egypt, an attitude spread to the Kuwaiti public through his speech on Kuwait Radio. The closing of government offices on the next day was the 'first mistake'. The US Consul's telegram to the Secretary of State on 4 February 1959 pointed out that the Deputy Ruler's position 'reflects to a great extent his increasing Nasserite prejudices'.[15]

This explanation was closely attuned to the prevailing Cold War attitudes in Washington, which were faithfully echoed in London. They did not take into account the potential consequences of a heavy-handed repression. The oilfields were very vulnerable to sabotage, and the earlier incidents with small bombs might have been repeated as a campaign on a vastly greater scale. This might have shut down oil production entirely, with disastrous economic consequences. Kuwait's public security forces were insufficient both to guard the oil network and to maintain public order in the urban areas at the same time. The alternative was too distasteful for Kuwaitis to contemplate: a complete takeover by British military forces.

The direct consequence of this crisis was intense political pressure on Abdullah Mubarak within the highest levels of government. Direct criticism of him was aired in a crisis meeting held by the Supreme Council chaired by the Emir, Sheikh Abdullah Al-Salem, who had shortened his visit to Lebanon and returned to Kuwait; Sheikh Fahad Al-Salem, a consistent critic, launched a personal attack on Sheikh Abdullah Mubarak (and by extension on his deputy, Sheikh Sabah Al-Ahmed) for encouraging the opposition. On the evening of 3 February, the Supreme Council held another meeting and adopted the resolutions, which Sheikh Abdullah Mubarak implemented, as the public security chief.[16]

On 4 February, Sheikh Abdullah Al-Salem issued an Emiri declaration that contained the following uncompromising words: 'I warn you once again to stop disturbing our relations with our friends and Arab brothers, as dictated by our homeland's interests. Ignore these stubborn youths who are blind to their country's interests.'[17]

The Public Security Department and the police also issued a statement:

> We remind you of His Highness The Emir's statement to his people. We would like to make clear that the Police and Security are vigilant and they are fully alert to safeguard the interest of the country. They will pursue whoever disturbs discipline, secretly or in public, and the Authority will never forgive those who do not listen to advice. We warn all people that the Authority will be very strict in protecting the interests of the community, which are superior to the interests of individuals. Serious consequences may follow.[18]

After restoring order, Abdullah Mubarak ordered the reopening of the clubs and asked Kuwaiti youths to keep them solely as venues for sports and social activities, and to keep away from demonstrations and illegal actions. His critics, however, led by Sheikh Fahad, remained much more powerful than they had been before.[19] Finally, on 7 February, the Emir issued a decree reorganizing government departments, merging the Public Security and Police Departments under Sheikh Abdullah

Mubarak's sole command.[20] This was a statement of official confidence in Abdullah Mubarak, and an act of closure. However, the matter was not closed. The political landscape had altered and, most serious of all, those within the government who were jealous of Abdullah Mubarak had shown their hand.

Abdullah Mubarak's riposte to the attacks made upon him was confident and effective. He said that this was a new situation emerging from the foreign invasion of Arab land. It was not going to disappear, and the events of early February 1959 had clearly shown that the security forces of Kuwait were too small and inadequately equipped to confront the new challenges faced by the state. Maintaining peace and security demanded a massive investment. Kuwait would threaten no other state, but it needed the capacity to respond to every likely threat. Kuwait would need a stronger army, a more effective naval presence and an air arm for all kinds of defensive role.

Abdullah Mubarak also emphasized that there were enemies within the state. He identified communist activities as a challenge to Kuwait, thereby prudently echoing the long-held attitudes of the United States and the British governments. These challenges had developed rapidly in Kuwait during the early 1950s. In particular, as the US Consular reports reveal, the US concern to pursue and to thwart 'communist activity' was unrelenting. This applied as much to ideas as to any directly subversive activity. It had a long history. In 1953, *Newsweek* published an analysis of some of the books issued in Beirut or Cairo and which had reached bookshops in Kuwait. The magazine claimed that the centre of communist activities had moved from Basra to Kuwait.[21] In the same month, however, the US Consulate in Kuwait wrote a report about the cooperation between the Public Security Department, Kuwait

Oil Company, American Oil Company and the British Political Agent, in fighting communist activities in Kuwait.

In 1954, a collection of translated communist-oriented books, issued by a Lebanese publishing house, appeared in Kuwait. On 29 May, the US Consulate sent a report to Washington about these books and reported the matter to the Political Agent and the Security Department. The report contained a list of the book titles, authors, translators and tables of contents. It identified the bookshops that were selling them. Initially, this issue did not attract much attention at the Public Security Department, and Abdullah Mubarak commented: 'No Arab will pay attention to these books.'[22] In the following year, a group of communists were arrested and interrogated, but even after thorough questioning they did not reveal the existence of any specific organization or any significant problem.[23]

In the same year, the US Consulate referred to leaflets issued by the National Committee for Peace Supporters in Kuwait calling for action in support of international peace. The British authorities expressed their anxiety that the leaflet had been distributed in Kuwait. However, as no copies of the leaflet were found in Kuwait, Abdullah Mubarak did not adopt any measures against the suspects.[24]

The US Consulate continued to pursue every pro-communist book or activity. In September of 1954, it wrote a report about communist organizations in Kuwait, referring to the communist activist Ahmad Al-Thaqqaf, a Palestinian, who issued a leaflet in the name of the head of the Kuwaiti communist cell (most members of the cell were non-Kuwaiti). The report linked this activity with communist movements in Syria and Iran.[25]

In 1954, the US Consulate prepared a report about communist books displayed at the Gulf Bookshop, run by

Yacoub Ali Yousef and Abdul Rahman Al-Rasheed. Such books included *The Soviet Doctrine in International Law* by S. Klerov, and Stalin's article 'The Dialectics and Historical Materialism' (1938) in his study *Problems of Leninism*. The report listed the press and publishing companies that issued these books in Baghdad. Again the possible presence of left-wing literature in Kuwait was enough to trigger alarm in Washington. In 1955, US anxiety about the threat of Marxist activity reached a new peak. In February, the US Consulate's assessment was that this activity was increasing and that the Kuwaiti authorities did not deal strongly enough with the growing danger. The US Consul sent 16 reports during the whole of 1954 on this issue, and then made six reports in January 1955 alone.[26] In April, a meeting was held between an official of the British Embassy in Washington and the State Department officials to exchange information on the apparently burgeoning communist activity in Kuwait.[27]

There was no let-up in 1956. Mr Gawain Bell, the British Political Agent, provided Abdullah Mubarak with information about the activities of local communists, based on reports of MI5 in Basra, which monitored the increased cooperation between communists in Iraq and Kuwait. On this occasion Abdullah Mubarak took the matter very seriously. He knew that the Iraqi Communist Party was seeking to penetrate Kuwait through Iraqis working there. Regular meetings were held between Abdullah Mubarak and the Public Security Department's advisor, Mr Coutts, who had previously worked for 24 years in the Sudanese police before being appointed as security advisor. Strenuous efforts were made by Abdullah Mubarak to counter these activities.[28] After some initial reluctance he initiated a series of arrests of known communists, stating his reason for delay to be that he thought it better to leave them in place but under close surveillance. This would expose their range of contacts and enable the government to destroy the entire network. However, the US Consulate demanded decisive action they could report to Washington rather than a string of intelligence reports. On 7 May 1956, police arrested 12 non-Kuwaiti communists, and 15 others were imprisoned later in May. This yielded no useful information, except what was already known, that the threat emanated from Iraq. On another occasion, an attempt to arrest 30 communists inside a house in the city failed because Abdul-Latif Faisal Al-Thuwaini, chief of domestic security, failed to react fast enough to the situation: Coutts complained to Sheikh Abdullah Mubarak, who was non-committal, and we must suspect that Al-Thuwaini was following Abdullah Mubarak's direct orders. Coutts's criticism of Al-Thuwaini's method of dealing with the communists grew louder: Al-Thuwaini summoned the suspects to the public security building, which Coutts claimed allowed them to get rid of any documents that might have implicated them. The alternative view was that this method would panic them into warning their network and lead to the exposure of the rest of their contacts.[29]

The Political Agent talked to Sheikh Abdullah Mubarak on this matter. He allayed Bell's doubts, pointing to the many cases of communist activity that the Public Security Department had managed to uncover entirely, without Coutts's knowledge or assistance. Abdullah Mubarak contrasted Coutts's heavy-handed methods, presumably learned during his career in the Sudan police, with the more up-to-date approach (in which the British Police Special Branch and British military intelligence (MI5) were highly skilled). What was important was not the number of communists in prison but the number still active and unknown to the police.

The Political Agent's response is unknown, but Abdullah Mubarak was so dismayed by the lack of trust displayed in him that he seriously considered resigning. It seemed that the British would invariably believe one of their own citizens rather than any Arab. However, both the Ruler of Kuwait, Sheikh Abdullah Al-Salem, and his Deputy Sheikh Abdullah Mubarak, regarded these British and US interventions as irrelevant and even harmful to Kuwait's interests. The purges were driven by an agenda set in Washington and London, to meet US and British political priorities.

The issue came to a head when Sir Bernard Burrows, the British Resident in the Gulf, raised the matter face-to-face with the Emir of Kuwait in March 1957. When he talked about the communist threat to Kuwait, the Emir responded by saying that communism was not a threat to Kuwait nor to any other state in the region. The Arab countries that co-operated with the Soviet Union did so to strengthen their negotiating position with the West. If his government received any confirmed information about any communist activity, he would deal with it firmly. The British Resident indicated in his report that the Emir would not address the issue of cooperation between the Public Security Department and the British security advisor. Sheikh Abdullah Mubarak expressed exactly the same sentiment as the Emir. When the British Resident raised the issue of the communist peril with him, Abdullah Mubarak deftly avoided the subject and moved on to discuss other issues.[30]

In 1958, the British opened a dialogue about a matter that was more relevant to Kuwait. They discussed the probable impact of the Iraqi revolution on the internal security of Kuwait. Several meetings were held between Abdullah Mubarak and the British military commanders in Bahrain. The British provided intelligence that showed pro-Iraqi elements were planning disturbances and expressed their readiness to use their forces in support of Kuwait. Some even suggested stationing troops in Kuwait as a precautionary measure. Abdullah Mubarak thanked them warmly and responded that his forces were capable of holding the airport and Al-Ahmadi port, until the arrival of British reinforcements.[31]

Kuwait's long-standing policy had been to maintain good relations with their larger neighbours – Saudi Arabia and Iraq. Abdullah Mubarak was anxious not to provoke the Qassem Government in Baghdad, so he asked the British authorities not to use Kuwait as the base for any retaliation against Iraq. The aim should be, he said, 'to keep Kuwait like a small Switzerland', not to be involved in the political conflicts between Britain and the new Iraqi regime. Despite the presence of Iraqi elements in the Kuwait Army, and the outbreak of demonstrations in Kuwait 10 days after the Iraqi revolution, the Public Security Department had dealt firmly with them before they could escalate.[32]

There were several attempts to normalize the relationship with Iraq. In 1959 an Iraqi Consular mission arrived in Kuwait to renew the passports of Iraqis living in Kuwait. Because the mission could not complete its work in time, its members were given an additional residence permit for one week. Abdullah Mubarak made it clear that they should finish their task and leave Kuwait immediately after that. When they applied for a further extension, Abdullah Mubarak agreed, provided the request came officially from the Iraqi authorities in Baghdad. A belated telegram from President Abdul Karim Qassem was sent to Sheikh Abdullah Mubarak asking him to grant the Iraqi mission one additional week. Abdullah Mubarak agreed, but placed the mission members under very close surveillance until their departure.

These attempts to improve relations with the new revolutionary government in Baghdad received a setback in April when Kuwait's Public Security Department launched a crackdown on communists. The Cairo newspaper *Al-Ahram* reported that Sheikh Abdullah Mubarak had ordered the deportation of 500 Iraqis who had recently arrived from Basra, and that their arrival in Kuwait 'was not for work as they claimed, but to sow the seeds of trouble and cause riots'.[33] However, Abdullah Mubarak was keen to put these events into a truer perspective by confirming that the normal condition in Kuwait was order and stability. Therefore, when the Middle East News Agency (MENA) reported an attempt of a communist coup in Kuwait, he immediately denied the report and summoned MENA's correspondent in Kuwait, insisting that the newspaper issue a retraction.[34] He also asked his friend Afif Al-Teebi, president of the Lebanese Journalists' Union, to publish a retraction in the Lebanese press.[35]

The most pressing concern in Kuwait during the later years of the 1950s was neither the border problems with Iraq nor the story of Kuwait's internal security and tranquility. The issue of Britain's future role in the nation's development could not be avoided. Sheikh Abdullah Mubarak had a strong admiration for individual Britons, and an equally strong liking for London and the British Isles. The constant problem for him was the belief inside the British Government that the United Kingdom should increase its activity and interest in Kuwait, largely on economic grounds, while the feeling in Kuwait was the precise opposite. Abdullah Mubarak completely recognized the benefit of Britain's protective role as a benign ally. What he could not stomach was the constant (and patronizing) British interference in the minutiae of Kuwait's internal affairs. This may explain why British reports are full of criticism of his sometimes-robust observations and slightly hostile demeanour.

We can sense his exasperation in his declaration late in 1959 that 'Kuwait will never become communist ... We are not fighting the communists alone. We fight them together with other Arab nations. Anyone who is deported leaves with respect; we do not confiscate his money; nothing happens to him; no oppression ... Whoever does not infringe our security will be able to live at peace in Kuwait.'[36] Over the years, Kuwait expelled communists originating from Jordan, Lebanon, Iraq and Iran without instructions from Britain or the US. They did so without rancour and without punishment. Abdullah Mubarak made sure that the members of the Iranian Communist Tudeh Party did not fall into the hands of the Shah's feared intelligence service, SAVAK.

The communist issue illustrates the narrowing gap between US and British priorities. British and US officials rigorously enforced the Cold War policies of their governments. Kuwait applied the standard that those who lived at peace in Kuwait and did not disturb the system of government were welcome to stay.

Certainly, by the beginning of June 1959, the Kuwaiti view was that communist activity was under full control.[37] The US Consul reported that Abdullah Mubarak announced on 7 June that the communist problem was over and that Kuwait was completely secure.[38] Nevertheless, the Public Security Department continued to monitor the publications coming from communist states and, in November, public security intercepted a large quantity of propaganda material (in Arabic) coming from China.

Communist propaganda was not the most dangerous thing smuggled into the country, although the British and US authorities sometimes gave that impression. The one import that Abdullah Mubarak considered much more harmful was narcotics. They threatened the health and future lives of Kuwaitis, so he gave the campaign against them his personal attention. Both the police and the Public Security Department clamped down on the smuggling channels and monitored traffickers. In 1954, a large quantity of opium was discovered aboard two ships coming from Aden.[39] Abdullah Mubarak asked Abdul-Latif Al-Thuwaini to trace the connection back to Aden; there he found a smuggling network with extensive international connections. The anti-narcotics campaign became a major commitment; in 1957, a member of an anti-smuggling unit was killed during the arrest of a smuggler. The efforts to guard the coastline were subsequently redoubled and the US Consulate reported approvingly to Washington that the Public Security Department was exerting great efforts in this regard; its secret agents covered the airport, the ports, along the border and other suspicious places in the city in order to stop any smuggling or trafficking operations. It was also noted that Abdullah Mubarak was so concerned with fighting narcotics that he had bought coastguard ships and high-speed launches to pursue smugglers offshore, as well as some helicopters for border surveillance.[40]

As a result of these efforts, narcotics did not, as Abdullah Mubarak had feared, become a major problem in Kuwait. The United Nations Mission that visited the country between 26 and 29 September 1959 discussed the measures adopted by Sheikh Abdullah Mubarak and was satisfied with the outcome. It concluded that the smuggling of narcotics to Kuwait did not constitute a major danger and was not comparable with the existing volume of trade in other countries such as Turkey or Lebanon.

§

One of the peculiarities of the legal system was that Sheikh Abdullah Mubarak had a judicial role. He acted as judge in disputes that concerned tribal law and custom, into which his early life gave him considerable insight. He was extremely courteous to the tribesmen who came before him or brought their disputes for his adjudication. He recognized that tribal justice was in some aspects different from the urban justice of Kuwait, and the most important matter was achieving an outcome that all the participants were able to accept. In that sense it was a special jurisdiction. Another form of jurisdiction that he resolutely opposed was the special courts that tried cases involving foreigners. These he considered unfair and providing unequal justice. It was a great satisfaction when an Emiri decree in February 1960 declared that special courts would be abolished and all residents of Kuwait would come within a single juridical structure. This, too, became an issue with Britain and the US who were anxious to maintain the special courts that favoured their citizens.

The decree of 1960 marked a shift in the relationship between Kuwait and the UK. The British policy had begun to change as it was recognized that the 1899 treaty was no longer operable. It was tacitly admitted by the Lord Privy Seal, Edward Heath, in 1961 that 'for some time past Kuwait had possessed entire responsibility for the conduct of its international relations and, with Britain's blessing, had joined a number of international organizations as a sovereign independent State'.[41] On 19 June 1960, there was a formal exchange of letters between the Emir and the Political Resident, Sir William Luce. The 1899 agreement was ended by mutual accord, and the letters stated, 'thereafter the relations between the two countries shall continue to be governed by a spirit of close friendship'. As Abdullah Mubarak had long realized, all that had stood between the continuing British and Kuwaiti friendship was Britain's strict interpretation of an outdated political relationship formed in the previous century.

The Key Institutions of
National Development

No modern state can survive or prosper without the capacity to defend its resources – in Kuwait's case, the oil reserves. Nor, as Abdullah Mubarak realized, could a twentieth-century state advance without a well-educated population. Then there are the symbols of most developing states such as a national airline, which the British dismissed as a preposterous and unnecessary luxury, yet in Kuwait's case the training of pilots for military service and for civil aviation served a dual function. In Kuwait these were not random, diverse elements but rather part of a coherent strategy for development.

Sheikh Abdullah Mubarak founded the Kuwait Defence Force in 1948. In 1949, he expressed his vision of building Kuwait's army and stated its objectives in the following terms: 'We, as Arabs and Muslims, have a deep-rooted heritage and traditions. We also have a past full of pride and glory; we have wishes and aspirations that we work to achieve by all available means. Today, in this troubled world, all peace-loving nations must strive to the maximum in adopting the necessary measures for defending their soil. Out of duty, and in accordance with the guidance of H.H. the Emir, I have laid the first brick in building a force, from the sons of this beloved homeland, to defend its soil and glorify its flag.'[1]

Abdullah Mubarak believed that the security of independent nations depends on their potential and their readiness to defend themselves. In practice, this meant that Kuwait, with its vast oil riches, could not afford to lose the British connection until it was able to protect itself. In 1954, the Emir appointed Abdullah Mubarak as the army's commander.[2] Ralph Hewins mentions that the building of the Kuwait Army, its modernization and increase in numbers, was entirely due to the efforts of Sheikh Abdullah Mubarak. From about 600 soldiers after World War II, the number increased to over 2,000 regular troops and numerous support units by the end of the 1950s.[3] His objective throughout had been simple: 'We will work hard to equip the emerging Kuwaiti Army with modern weapons and equipment.'[4]

In 1957, according to US documents, Abdullah Mubarak adopted two important measures for modernizing the army's equipment. The first was inviting General Sir Geoffrey Kemp Bourne, Chief of Staff of the British Land Forces in the Middle East, to visit Kuwait. Abdullah Mubarak organized a military parade involving 1,000 men of the border forces and 1,500 men of the security forces. The second was a request to the British Government to purchase 6,000 modern rifles and machine guns.[5] According to the US Consul's report on General Bourne's visit: 'The General, after inspecting the troops, recommended the purchase of the arms which are suitable for desert war and gave an example of what happened to the Iraqi Army which lost numerous tanks because of the technical faults resulting from their unsuitability for a desert climate. He also indicated the need for a number of British trainers to upgrade the army's technical efficiency.'[6]

US documents mention that, during the period between 16 and 18 March 1958, Abdullah Mubarak observed the army's exercises accompanied by the Political Agent, who described the exercises as 'very good' and reported that the soldiers were physically fit and highly alert.[7] The report also commented on Abdullah Mubarak's excellent personal relations with his officers. A report by the US Consul indicated that, during an army exercise, the exceptional performance of one of the officers attracted Abdullah Mubarak's attention. He called him immediately and on the spot nominated him for a tank warfare course in the UK.[8] This was the same morale-building approach that he had adopted in building the civilian government services. He recognized that a cadre of loyal, hardworking and efficient young men was the key to building successful institutions.

A professional full-time army was a novelty in Kuwait and Abdullah Mubarak had to persuade the people that it should be the prime focus for national pride. He decided to institute a medium for communication between the army and the people. He persuaded newspaper editors to give full coverage of every important event that featured the armed forces, and ordered the creation of a magazine about the army, the navy and, later, the air force. The first issue of *Humat Al-Watan* magazine was issued in October 1960, introducing itself as 'The Magazine of the Army and the Armed Forces'. In its first issue, he wrote an editorial explaining the reasons for issuing the magazine, saying: 'As the interests of this country require continuing efforts in upgrading the cultural and military levels in Kuwait, the people need to know of the progress of its brave Army, so we decided to publish this military magazine focusing on Army affairs.'[9]

The magazine's first issues contained various military studies and cultural, social and religious articles. It was not restricted to military information. In every volume it published a poem, a story, an article about a battle from the history of Kuwait or of the Arabs, and Qur'anic verses and Prophet's sayings (Ahadith). The first issue, for instance, contained military articles such as the role of armoured units in modern wars, cooperation between the infantry and field artillery, the army's security service, air surveillance, nuclear weapons and radio communications. In order to enhance the spirit of solidarity between soldiers and civilians, the magazine published an article entitled: 'A letter from a soldier to his mother' and another article on the sea battle of Al-Reqqa. It also published a report illustrated in colour on the graduation of the first batch of commandos for the Kuwait Army.

The second issue, published in November 1960, contained military studies about tanks in battle, defensive fighting, field skills training, army engineers and helicopters. On military history, it published an article on 'Khaled Ibn Al Walid's heroic acts'. Another article was 'Women are the pillars of renaissance', whose writer emphasized the significant role of women in the progress of societies. The writers published in *Humat Al-Watan* were some of the best known in Kuwait, as well as Arabs from other countries. They include Abdul Razzak Al-Basir, Dr Suhail Idris, Dr Qadri Hafez Toukan and Dr Nicola Ziyada. From March 1961, the magazine issued a supplement entitled 'Here is Kuwait', containing a monthly list of Kuwait's radio programmes, with brief reviews and excerpts.

In 1945, the British Army had published the first monthly issue of *SOLDIER* magazine, on the orders of the commander-in-chief, Field Marshal Montgomery. It was distributed free to all serving soldiers, and regular market research proved that it was remarkably successful at building high morale among soldiers and a positive impression among its civilian readership. We cannot know if it was the model for *Humat Al-Watan*, but every British soldier in Kuwait would have received a copy. *Humat Al-Watan* certainly achieved a similar success to *SOLDIER*, by becoming the 'house magazine' of the armed forces.

§

Morale is essential for every successful army, but Abdullah Mubarak knew that the most pressing need of the Kuwaiti Army was for the best and most modern arms and equipment. This applied to all three branches of the armed forces: land forces, air and navy. The story of the army's development has yet to be written, although British and US documents contain a version of the story of the Kuwaiti need for munitions and a wide range of equipment, and Sheikh Abdullah Mubarak's role in the development. There is also a clear record of Britain laying obstacles in the path of many of the arms purchases, the long negotiations that Abdullah Mubarak had to undertake to obtain arms, as well as London's fear that he would attempt to obtain weapons from other sources.[10] There are also indications that sometimes the British advice was better than Abdullah Mubarak's own non-professional preferences.

The main object of Abdullah Mubarak's visit to Britain in May 1956 was to establish a successful bilateral military relationship. According to British documents, he visited Britain regularly, most often to secure military equipment for the Kuwait Army.[11] In return, London exerted pressure on him to appoint a British advisor to the army, to use British officers as instructors for the Kuwaiti security forces, and to employ British technicians for the maintenance of modern military equipment.

The question of arms supply had a history before 1956.[12] During his 1951 visit, Abdullah Mubarak's top priority had been to buy 10 armoured vehicles for public security, and he managed to sign the contract just before his departure. It is clear that the British Government's approval only came after it was assured of Abdullah Mubarak's competence in managing public security in Kuwait.[13]

A wholehearted admirer of the British armed forces, Abdullah Mubarak respected their skill and sophistication, and the officers he met were intelligent, well informed and respectful. British officers treated him as a brother officer. This was the reason he raised no objection to the idea of appointing a British military advisor to the Kuwaiti Army.

However, this seemingly simple act had roots back to September 1950. The Political Agent, Herbert Jenkins, had seized the opportunity of Sheikh Abdullah Mubarak's visit to Beirut for medical treatment to raise the issue with the Emir of appointing a military advisor for the army. The Emir recommended postponing any discussions of this matter until Abdullah Mubarak's return, and asked the Political Agent to discuss the matter directly with him, as the responsible minister.[14] Yet no further action was taken and the Political Agent did not talk to Abdullah Mubarak as the Emir had suggested.

A year later, in September 1951, Jenkins again raised the issue with the Emir. He answered, according to the Political Agent's report, very firmly that he would not agree to appoint a military advisor without Sheikh Abdullah Mubarak's express approval; otherwise, Abdullah Mubarak would resign and create a crisis within the family.[15]

Jenkins saw in the clash between the Kuwaiti and Iraqi border forces in 1954 a new opportunity to raise the issue of increasing the power of the Kuwaiti border force. The event confirmed in his view the necessity for British control over this force by appointing Britons to work with it, a plan that Abdullah Mubarak now strongly opposed.[16] It was now clear that the US Government was happy to sell arms to Kuwait, without the tangle of regulations that the British wanted to impose. Sheikh Abdullah Mubarak's request to purchase more weapons was approved in Washington on 14 July 1956, and the weapons were shipped 12 days later.[17]

This was a great embarrassment for the British Government. The deal had been under discussion at the Foreign Office for a long period, and it was at a late stage that an official wrote in January 1956: 'The arms requested exceed the anticipated needs of the Public Security forces; but the Emir did not try to reduce them and approved Abdullah Mubarak's requests without amendment.'[18] Now the US Government had shown its willingness to become the supplier of choice to Kuwait without any of the questioning and pettifogging regulation that accompanied every British concession. The economic implications were very serious: Britain might lose the valuable Kuwaiti market.

The failure focused British Government attention on the advice emanating from the Political Agency in Kuwait. The Political Agent's reports had raised several questions about the real objective for Sheikh Abdullah Mubarak to develop the public security forces. An explanation had been put forward that he aimed at creating a 'Power Centre' to support him in any forthcoming struggle in power. Yet there was no evidence whatever offered to support this supposition. From this point onwards, the government in London read the Political Agent's report with much greater circumspection.

A new Political Agent, Gawain Bell, had been appointed in 1955 and had struggled with Abdullah Mubarak over the supposed communist threat. The real fear, however – that Kuwait would in future seek its arms from the United States – proved groundless. In November 1957, Abdullah Mubarak requested the supply of 6,000 small arms during the reception for General Geoffrey Kemp Bourne, Chief of Staff of the British Middle East Land Forces, and he also sought to obtain vehicles for military use. When the British authorities raised, yet again, the idea of sending British advisors to train the Kuwaiti forces in the use of these weapons, Abdullah Mubarak was not enthusiastic and asserted that his forces could use and maintain them.[19] In this case, the British wisely chose to let the matter rest.

There is no doubt that Abdullah Mubarak looked upon British military support as an essential guarantee of Kuwaiti independence. After the Iraqi revolution, Iraq's policies often threatened Kuwait's security and stability. In that perilous situation, Abdullah Mubarak accepted the appointment of a British advisor to the Kuwait Army; however, he insisted that he himself should select the advisor. He chose Major Tom Pierce, who had earlier come to Kuwait to train artillery officers. For a while, the British Government was reluctant to accept an arrangement that would prevent it from choosing the advisor. However, the new Political Agent, Aubrey Halford-Macleod, was afraid that any British reservation might lead to Sheikh Abdullah Mubarak revoking his approval. He sensibly wrote to London suggesting to the Foreign Office to accept the Pierce appointment, which it eventually approved.[20]

Between 1959 and 1961, as it became clear that the treaty with Britain might be in its last phase, Abdullah Mubarak worked hard to conclude a number of arms deals. In 1959, he worked to increase the size of the Kuwait Army, upgrade its training, and develop a stock of arms and equipment. Intensive training was implemented in the use of this equipment in emergency situations. The Kuwait Army conducted a large-scale exercise for this purpose in which, according to the Political Agent, the army performed well.

In May 1959, Abdullah Mubarak requested the purchase of a number of Centurion tanks and a large quantity of anti-aircraft and anti-tank weapons, light troop carriers and communications equipment. Britain made its approval conditional on the appointment of British advisors and technicians to maintain the equipment and to train the Kuwaitis.[21]

On 12 June 1959, the US Ambassador in London sent a telegram to the Department of State in Washington saying that the British Government had decided, in principle, to respond to Kuwait's request for tanks and anti-aircraft weapons and that the agreement involved dispatching a team of British technicians to train the Kuwaitis, provided that Britain was satisfied that the Ruler approved of the armament plan proposed by Sheikh Abdullah Mubarak.[22] The stress here was on 'decided in principle'; if, as seemed possible, the British Government decided against granting the request, then Abdullah Mubarak would inevitably come knocking on the doors of the US State Department.

London did not want to strengthen the armament of the Kuwait Army and attempted to frustrate the Kuwaiti demands. This must be taken in the context of the fact that the treaty arrangement seemed likely to come to an end. The British documents for 1960–1 fully cover Abdullah Mubarak's negotiations for an arms deal to develop the Kuwait Navy and to purchase sophisticated military aircraft. He was also interested in modernizing the navy, especially as the activity of the coast guard in the protection of Kuwait's territorial waters was among the armed forces' main responsibilities as a result of illegal infiltration from the sea. The British documents indicate that Abdullah Mubarak frequently talked with the Political Agent and the British Royal Navy representative about the importance of obtaining fast patrol boats and the patrol aircraft to monitor the coasts, combat smuggling and to supervise the security of remote areas. It seems very likely that the British Government was seeking to establish some vestige of continuing control over an uncertain future.

The nature of these negotiations was different from those that had gone before. A report dated 3 February 1961 said that the assessment of the British Admiralty was that the required boats were not available but they could be built specially for Kuwait. It sent the Political Agent a list of the British companies that he could, if he approved, deliver to Abdullah Mubarak.[23]

On 9 February, the British Admiralty wrote again to the Foreign Office reaffirming that the ships to meet the Kuwaiti specification were not available.[24] There were other boats in Malta and Abdullah Mubarak might send his representatives to check their suitability. There was also one boat type called the Bold Class Fast Attack Boat that the British Royal Navy had used for a short time, but the report warned against its maintenance problems and the scarcity of spare parts for its innovative gas turbines. The implication was that if the Kuwaitis wanted to make their own arrangements for British equipment, let them do so, and they would see that it was not as easy as they had imagined.

Sheikh Abdullah Mubarak was not convinced with this response and considered it an attempt to prevent Kuwait from obtaining advanced weapons. The war of nerves continued. On 18 February, Colonel Mubarak al-Abdullah Al-Jaber informed the Political Agent that Sheikh Abdullah Mubarak wanted his intervention, as well as that of the Foreign Office, to convince the Admiralty to provide Kuwait with the ships. The Political Agent repeated the previous position, and concluded his report with a remark that Abdullah Mubarak's position reflected his doubts about the truthfulness of the British statement. The Political Agent confirmed to Sheikh Abdullah Mubarak the non-availability of these ships from the Admiralty and that he had requested more information about, and a picture of, the Bold Class vessel and its location so that Kuwait could send a team to inspect it. He also told Abdullah Mubarak that building a vessel would take two years and that he could directly contact the manufacturing companies so that one of them might agree to build one for Kuwait.[25]

The issue of aircraft supply was much more serious. Abdullah Mubarak exerted an extraordinary effort and entered into tough negotiations with the British Government to obtain armed Jet Provost trainer aircraft.

The reports of the Political Agent show that the issue dated back to March 1960 when Abdullah Mubarak decided to buy six jet training aircraft with combat capability.[26] Quite why he had settled on the Jet Provost as a dual-purpose aircraft to satisfy Kuwait's needs is unclear. Most Jet Provosts were used as unarmed basic training aircraft. Even the armed version was no match for the new MIG-17 fighter supplied to Iraq's air force. On 6 February 1961, the Foreign Office informed the Political Agent in Kuwait that Sheikh Abdullah Mubarak had asked the assistant to the Ruler's Representative in Kuwait's London office to contact the manufacturing company and obtain a quotation.[27]

The assistant did indeed negotiate with Hunting Percival Aircraft Ltd, the makers of this type of aircraft. He also contacted the War Office to provide the necessary training for pilots. The British authorities seemed uncertain of Sheikh

Abdullah Mubarak's seriousness in concluding this deal. Therefore, they approved the request provided that the agreement was signed by a fixed date. A report by the Foreign Office to the Political Agent dated 6 February stated that three aircraft could be delivered in June and three more in July, provided the agreement had been signed no later than 15 February.[28] In other words, the Ministry gave Abdullah Mubarak nine days to discuss the contract details, including its financial and structural aspects, and to sign it.

Pilot training would not prove difficult because 13 Kuwaiti pilots who were training in London had previous civil flight experience, which would facilitate their training on military jets. They could then fly the aircraft to Kuwait in June. Abdullah Mubarak followed the pilots' training programmes personally, and made a decision to terminate the scholarship of any who failed without an acceptable excuse.

A report by the War Office said that because these aircraft were not in service with the Royal Air Force, training should take place in Kuwait – and it was prepared to delegate one of its officers for a short period, but that if the Kuwaitis still 'do not welcome the idea', the manufacturing company could use the expertise of a retired officer.[29] On 11 February, the British official responsible for the negotiations (Polglese) notified Hunting Percival Aircraft of Sheikh Mubarak Abdullah's acceptance of its offer, provided the aircraft John would arrive in Kuwait before the end of June 1961 with the minimum number of maintenance teams.[30] (Note: Sheikh Abdullah Mubarak set 19 June 1961 as the delivery date, which was Kuwait's independence day.) The company should organize the training of 13 Kuwaiti pilots who would fly the aircraft to Kuwait, and the aircraft should be prepared as fighter aircraft rather than for a training role. The contract should also contain some penalties in case the company failed to comply with the agreed dates.

On 2 March, Polglese left for Beirut to meet Abdullah Mubarak and inform him of the latest developments. In the Foreign Office report, based on the information provided by Polglese, Abdullah Mubarak appeared extremely upset and accused the British Government of lacking any desire to sell modern weapons to Kuwait.[31] Polglese mentioned that it was the worst meeting ever with Abdullah Mubarak, who was furious.

In the letter from Polglese to Abdullah Mubarak on 8 March, he mentioned that the Air Ministry would be unable to equip the aircraft with the required guns on the agreed dates: moreover the available guns were Browning .50 calibre cannon, and not the .303 machine guns specified.[32] Polglese suggested changing the aircraft type and advised Kuwait to consider buying the Hunter fighter aircraft. He explained the Hunter's advantages, saying that they were designed for use as fighter and ground-attack aircraft and were in use by the British forces in Aden, which would facilitate maintenance, technical supervision and obtaining spare parts. Polglese added that if Abdullah Mubarak agreed, the aircraft could be delivered within 12 months, perhaps less. The Air Ministry would provide every possible assistance to conclude the deal. He added that the Ministry would like to know the probable use of the aircraft and whether Kuwait would use them for pursuit, training or ground attack and what communications equipment would be required. Each of these roles required special equipment and systems. This was essential information, which the Kuwaitis had failed to supply. The Ministry also requested a training programme for the Kuwaiti pilots. Polglese mentioned that the Air Ministry believed a number of practical, technical and administrative problems existed, which required serious consideration. Therefore, it suggested sending one of its officers to Kuwait to discuss these issues. He asked Abdullah Mubarak to accept the offer, stating: 'I believe it represents the safest means to safeguard your interests and to obtain the best results.'

In the report of the Political Agent to the Foreign Office on 14 March, he said that Abdullah Mubarak had accepted the War Ministry's offer regarding training and he would decide on its venue, either in the UK or Kuwait.[33] But he refused the idea of changing the aircraft type and buying Hunters instead of Provosts. Abdullah Mubarak described what was happening as blackmail and unacceptable pressure to buy the Hunters, seemingly not having considered the far superior performance and armament of the Hunter aircraft in an air defence or ground-attack role.

Once again, Polglese tried to convince Abdullah Mubarak to change his mind. On 22 March, he sent a telegram saying he had received no reply to his telegram of 8 March and that he had visited the Kuwaiti pilots who were being trained at an RAF unit near Nottingham.[34] Training was being carried out according to schedule and, he said, 'All are outstanding and working hard; their instructors commend them and do not expect any difficulty in finalizing their training on flying their aircraft by the end of July.' Training for the fighter plane needed one further month, he added.

Polglese went back once again to the idea of buying the Hunters. Training to use them would require less than 12 months and the Air Ministry was ready to offer any possible help and to send a negotiating team by mid-April.

Yet Abdullah Mubarak remained adamant. At the end of March he sent his military advisor, Colonel Pierce, to London to meet with Polglese and to visit Hunting Percival Aircraft Ltd and the Air Ministry, and to familiarize himself with the best weapons with which to equip the aircraft.[35] Indeed, Pierce visited the Ministry, accompanied by Polglese, on 30 March.[36] He confirmed the selection of the Provosts and discussed the appropriate weapons. He obtained confirmation from the Air Ministry of its readiness to supply the spare parts and ammunition for the aircraft's guns and that the planes would be delivered to Kuwait in the summer of 1961. Upon his return, Pierce confirmed to Abdullah Mubarak that the Jet Provosts were best for the Kuwaiti forces and the Browning .303 machine gun was the best armament for the aircraft. Abdullah Mubarak accepted Pierce's suggestions and issued his orders to go ahead with concluding the deal.[37] It should be remembered that Pierce was an artillery officer, with no experience of fighter aircraft. He was also aware of Abdullah Mubarak's strong preference for the Jet Provosts.

It might appear that the British attitude was characterized by procrastination and the stubborn desire to change the type of the aircraft. In fact, there were good reasons for suggesting the Hunter. Since the Jet Provosts would be used primarily in a fighter role, they were much less suitable than the Hunters which were designed for that role. The reason that the guns specified for these aircraft were not in stock was because British fighter aircraft had now moved over to ADEN cannon as their armament.

The statement that the required training period was too long may or may not have been true; but the unavailability of spare parts was certainly true because the fighter version of the Jet Provost was not in service with the Royal Air Force.

To Abdullah Mubarak it seemed that the British political decision was not in favour of concluding the deal. He was largely correct. According to John Richmond, the Political Agent, on 21 March 1961: 'There is a conflict between the British political, economic and military interests and Abdullah Mubarak's demands.' He indicated that 'the arrival of these planes will tilt the internal balance of powers contrary to our interests'.[38] While Britain welcomed the building and equipping of aviation facilities to receive jet planes at Kuwait airport, building a Kuwaiti jet air force was not what Britain wanted. However, it is unclear what Britain wanted at this stage, for three months later Kuwait achieved its independence.

On 29 April, the Political Agent received a letter accepting the aircraft deal with Hunting Percival according to the 10 April offer. The director of the Eastern Department of the Ministry expressed his surprise at the continuation of the deal after Sheikh Abdullah Mubarak's resignation.[39] But the Kuwaiti position then changed and new instructions to cancel the deal arrived at the end of June 1961.[40] What role, if any, the confused situation over the aircraft supply may have played in Abdullah Mubarak's decision to resign must remain uncertain. However, it was certainly the most ill-managed procurement process, on both sides, in the whole history of Anglo-Kuwaiti arms sales. It was also probably the most important. The attempt to cancel the contract failed and four Jet T51 armed trainers were eventually bought.[41] Yet in 1964, the Kuwait Air Force equipped with Hawker Hunters, followed in 1971 with the English Electric Lightning aircraft. Thereafter, Kuwait turned to France and the USA for their air defence equipment.

Civil aviation

Abdullah Mubarak's commitment to the development of aviation was probably the most far-sighted of all his policies.

The close personal attention he gave to the first military aircraft for Kuwait indicates the great importance he attached to this development. He believed that air power would be crucial in the region, and this was not merely the aircraft but the pilots as well. It was for this reason that he encouraged the development of civil aviation: many of the pilots for the embryonic Kuwaiti Air Force had first learned their skills at the aviation club or from flying civil aircraft.

With the increased importance of air communication in the 1940s, and with Iraqi and Egyptian airlines linking Beirut and Cairo with Kuwait, Abdullah Mubarak established a Civil Aviation Department, an international airport, a national airline and an aviation club and school.

At the beginning, Britain was unenthusiastic about a Civil Aviation Department in Kuwait, but this did not discourage Abdullah Mubarak. A report to Washington in mid-March 1953 described Sheikh Abdullah Mubarak opening the 'Kuwait Club and Aviation School' with a large celebration, which the leading figures in Kuwait attended. The school had bought four Auster training aircraft from Britain and the club had rooms inside the airport building. The school was managed by Mustafa Sadeq, the aviation chief at the Public Security Department, who was assisted by three pilots – one British and two Egyptian – who were entrusted with training and aircraft maintenance.[42]

Officers from the Public Security Department were the first group to be seconded for flight training. All wore a pilot's uniform modelled on that of British Royal Air Force pilots, but with Kuwait badges.[43] In May 1954, two club members passed their final air flight tests, and on 20 December 1954 Abdullah Mubarak attended the graduation of the first batch of Kuwaiti pilots.[44] It was a moment of great pride. During the celebration, he announced that the pilots were leaving for England in March

1955 to undergo advanced flight training. With these early successes, the club soon attracted a number of able young Kuwaitis, who later became the nucleus of Kuwaiti Air Company and the Kuwait Air Force. In light of the continuing success of the Kuwaiti Aero Club, the British Aero Clubs and Centres awarded Abdullah Mubarak 'Honorary Wings' (the pilot's insignia) at a grand celebration in Kuwait.[45] He appreciated the honour and the mark of recognition it gave to the development of Kuwaiti aviation.

In contrast to this success, it appears that the British Foreign Office had received 'troubling information' that made it suspicious of the club and its prospects. A report from the Foreign Office to the Political Agent, in June 1954, mentioned that the club's name in Arabic was 'Kuwait Air', which to London indicated that Abdullah Mubarak might be thinking ahead into making the club into the nucleus of a Kuwaiti Air Force. Instructions were sent to the Political Agent to monitor in secret the club's activities.[46] In 1959, he reported that the club had two up-to-date Dove and eight Auster training aircraft. Its training programmes also developed and reached the level of awarding a civil pilot's licence.[47]

The Aero Club certainly considered establishing a civilian Kuwait Air Company;[48] and Abdullah Mubarak strenuously encouraged Abdul Razzak Jamil Qaddoumi in his ambition to establish an aviation business. A report to the US State Department from the Consulate explained that the rapprochement between Abdullah Mubarak and the Syrian Government in early 1953 was prompted by Kuwait's desire to benefit from the Syrian expertise in civil aviation, a desire 'which Britain strongly detested', according to the report.[49]

According to US documents, preparations for establishing Kuwait Airways began in 1953, with the main role played by

Sheikh Abdullah Mubarak, assisted by Abdul Razzak Qaddoumi who obtained the licence. He started negotiations to establish the company following the Syrian model[50] and, on 16 March 1954, National Kuwait Airways Ltd celebrated the arrival of its first plane, named *Kazma* (an ancient name for Kuwait). On 18 March the company began regular flights to Basra, Bahrain and Beirut.[51]

The same year, 1954, Qaddoumi established Arabian Desert Airlines, with Abdullah Mubarak providing bank guarantees to set up the new venture. The company had two planes and operated the routes between Kuwait and Beirut, Bahrain, Damascus and Jerusalem.[52] According to an American report it went out of business in 1959,[53] but in reality Qaddoumi sold the company to Sheikh Duaij Al-Salman, who developed its business and operated regular flights to Cairo, Beirut, Damascus, Qatar and Bahrain until 1961.

In 1958, an official national carrier, Kuwait Airways, was established with regular routes between Kuwait and Beirut, Basra, Jerusalem, Dhahran, Cairo and Doha. It recruited experienced staff from other airlines to supply technical and administrative expertise; negotiations with a Lebanese company ended after Sheikh Abdullah Mubarak objected to the high profit margin it demanded for its services. Extensive efforts began to link Kuwait into the world aviation network. The company tried to reach an agreement with the American West Air Transport, but without success. It had no greater success with the two main US airlines, Pan American and Trans World Airlines (TWA), to extend their networks to Kuwait. Abdullah Mubarak asked the US Consul to request the State Department to advance the case of American Airlines serving the Kuwait market, offering favourable terms for what he described as a market with bright future prospects. That too was unsuccessful.

In the end it was BOAC (British Overseas Airways Corporation) that finally agreed on 1 June 1958 to extend their network to Kuwait. Abdullah Mubarak might have preferred a US airline as Kuwait's primary link to the outside world, but he was happy in the end to accept the British offer. It was a well-thought-out plan, with real enthusiasm from BOAC. He signed the contract as the acting Ruler, since the Emir was out of the country at the time.[54] It proved a very satisfactory arrangement to both parties, giving Kuwait easy access to the world market via London. At the same time, Kuwait Airways was flourishing. In April 1959 it had two regular flights to Bombay, via Doha and Karachi. In May, it opened another route to London via Cairo, Tripoli and Nice. In 1962, it rented a Comet jet aircraft but the aircraft was eventually withdrawn after the aircraft type proved unsafe. Six years later Kuwait Airways, by then 100 per cent owned by the state, bought its first Boeing 707 aircraft, and ten years later was operating a large fleet of the latest Boeing aircraft to long-range international destinations.

The expansion of civil aviation required an institution to manage the sector. On 1 October 1956, Sheikh Abdullah Mubarak, in his capacity as the Ruler's deputy, announced the establishment of the Civil Aviation Department, under his control. On 10 October, he appointed Mustafa Sadeq, the manager of Kuwait Aero Club, as director of Civil Aviation and Administrative Affairs. He replaced James Forrest, the British advisor for civil aviation, although Forrest retained overall responsibility for technical matters.[55] The US Consulate noted that the establishment of a Civil Aviation Department was well received by Kuwaitis as a sign of their country's growing standing within the international community.[56]

Abdullah Mubarak had recognized that Kuwait would need to play its part at the international level, where the future of the world's civil aviation was discussed and negotiated. From the beginning, Kuwait had agreed to follow British aviation practice and regulation: two formal agreements were signed, the first on 5 September 1950 and the second on 31 March 1956, with the British air attaché, Beverly Barnard, suggesting a number of new operational controls for Kuwait's civil aviation, bringing it fully into line with British practice. In 1958, the British Political Agent presented an English copy of the full proposals to Abdullah Mubarak, who asked Mustafa Sadeq to translate and apply them, a task that he had completed by the end of the year.

When Abdullah Mubarak authorized Mustafa Sadeq to introduce a registration system for Kuwaiti planes, the latter developed a comprehensive structure for civil aviation that regulated aircraft registration rules as well as taking overall control of the registration process. This was based on a study of international best practice. Abdullah Mubarak approved this and issued a law in December 1958,[57] which he signed as the head of public security and civil aviation.

The British authorities objected, however, since this new system departed from current British practice, and the new law also conflicted with the bilateral agreement of 1956. For instance, the law gave Kuwait the right to permit foreign aircraft to use Kuwait Airport, a right that Britain wanted to keep for itself. When the British air attaché clarified the position, and demonstrated that the new regulations were not in accord with the 1956 agreement, Abdullah Mubarak did not amend them but said that he recognized the 'error' and they would delay implementation of the law in view of its conflict with the bilateral agreement.[58] Nothing more was done.

This chapter has so far stated the facts pertaining to the civil aviation rules as they appear in the relevant documents. They do not, however, reveal the whole story. One should reflect on Mustafa Sadeq's behaviour: did he ignore Abdullah Mubarak's instructions in translating the British proposals? Or could he only make the changes in accordance with the Sheikh's personal instructions? We must wonder about the new rules that gave more power to the Kuwaiti authorities: could Sadeq make such changes without Abdullah Mubarak's authority? Was there an 'error' at all? The explanation may be found in Abdullah Mubarak's reaction to the British complaint. He did not annul the new regulations; he would only ensure that they would not be implemented in a way that 'conflicted' with the 1956 agreement. In this way, he shrewdly satisfied the British without committing himself to any specific course of action.

During the 1950s, Sheikh Abdullah Mubarak showed great interest in building a new airport as the existing one was in an unsatisfactory state. A US Consulate report stated in 1954 that the development committee had approved the new airport project, and plans were made to obtain the necessary land. Costs of the planned project were estimated at £5 million. Completion was to take place over two years, and the project was open to international tender.[59]

The British authorities insisted on approving the specific-ation and the building procedures. However, the necessary assessments were repeatedly postponed and the project had to be put on hold. Abdullah Mubarak again took up the matter with British officials and expressed his great dissatisfaction at the inexplicable (and he believed unjustifiable) delay. A report of the British Political Agent in 1956 stated that Abdullah Mubarak was very 'eager to start the construction of the new airport as soon as possible', and that 'he was unhappy with the condition of the runway and the airport buildings which do not suit a country like Kuwait ... construction works should not be delayed any further'. The Political Agent expressed his satisfaction with Abdullah Mubarak's competence in managing the civil aviation sector.[60]

On 9 November 1957, Abdullah Mubarak, in his capacity as director of the Civil Aviation Department, signed an agreement with Wing Commander Lawes, the representative of International Air Ltd, the company that organized the development work for the new airport and provided the technical supervision of the airport services and facilities.[61] Britain did not view these developments with any great enthusiasm. The Foreign Office preferred to minimize Kuwaitis' access to the outside world and to ensure that external contracts would be made through London and thus under its supervision. Therefore, when Scandinavian Airlines (SAS) applied for permission to open a route to Kuwait, Britain, as the supervisor of Kuwait's foreign relations, recommended rejection of the request.[62]

A report published in *Al-Kuwait Al-Youm* in December 1958 reflected Abdullah Mubarak's vision for developing civil aviation. He defined the department's objectives as: to draw up a long-term policy for airports; ensure the safety of all air traffic; and recruit and train the necessary technicians and air transportation staff. The policy would include the supervision of airports, air training-schools and flying clubs. Kuwait would create comprehensive legislation to cover all aspects of civil aviation and work in cooperation with other countries. Certainly, Kuwait was scrupulous in fulfilling all its international accords. A Kuwaiti Navigation and Aviation Register law was enacted that made it a requirement for all aircraft to have registration marks plus call signs for all registered planes. A new aircraft runway was built and a new long-range wireless station established. Young Kuwaitis were sent abroad to obtain the necessary jet aircraft training and certification. As for the Aviation Academy, the report indicates that 17 Kuwaitis were awarded the special flight certificate; 90 pilots flew independently, 11 of whom were sent abroad and 5 of whom obtained the highest commercial aviation certificate. The report highlighted the role of the flying club in fulfilling responsibilities beyond training. Its pilots and training aircraft helped to monitor Kuwait's border in times of emergency, took aerial photographs of Kuwait and participated in aerial spraying programmes against disease and infection.[63]

Sheikh Abdullah Mubarak pioneered civil aviation in Kuwait, often in the face of international opposition. His efforts began with founding the airway company, building the new airport and opening the flying club to provide the basic training for Kuwaiti pilots to fly the national airline's planes. Aviation and a national airline were regarded worldwide as the most powerful emblems of modernity, and Kuwait's rapid development was good evidence that the nation had taken a substantial step forward. Every time that an airliner in the livery of Kuwait landed at or took off from an airport in North America, Europe or Asia, it was a symbol of Kuwait's growing status. Its smart new aircraft offered excellent service and had a reputation for high quality, thus giving Abdullah Mubarak a feeling of deep satisfaction.

Education in Kuwait

Regarding education as one of Kuwait's key strategic assets, Abdullah Mubarak had campaigned for educational progress for even longer than he had championed aviation.[64] As chairman of the Education Council he had the status and authority to push hard for progress. Truly modern education in

Kuwait began in the second half of the 1940s, when the Kuwaiti Government developed secondary education and sent students abroad for tertiary education.[65] The first university educational mission was to Egypt in 1939. It included Abdul Aziz Hussein, who was first administrator of Kuwait's House in Cairo (the building that became Kuwait's embassy after independence in 1961). Abdul Aziz Hussein became director of education in 1952.[66]

We can trace the detailed development of education from the minutes of the Education Council's meetings, as published by the newspaper *Kuwait Al-Youm*. These local records indicate the great range of Abdullah Mubarak's contribution to educational development. In its meeting of 3 May 1955, for instance, the Council under his chairmanship endorsed new contracts for teachers; established guidelines for a series of lectures; and approved the Department of Education's measures to provide drinking water to all village schools. It also discussed the memorandum for Kuwait's participation in the International Scout Camp in Canada. The Council approved the participation, provided it was 'in Kuwait's name, and not to be in association with another State'.[67]

In its 4 December 1955 meeting, the Council discussed building a 'Kuwait House' on the land purchased by the Education Department at Al-Duqqi in Cairo.[68] In its next session it approved the secretary's proposal to hold its session at 8.30 a.m. every Sunday; and in its 27 December session it discussed the need for Kuwait's Education Department to participate in UNESCO in order to become acquainted with the educational development and cultural trends of the advanced countries. The Council approved the proposal,[69] and in its report stressed that it would represent 'Kuwait's protection from any foreign danger or internal contagion. A healthy society requires first and foremost getting rid of ignorance and bringing in enlightenment of the mind.' Clearly Abdullah Mubarak saw educational development in the same way that he regarded the armed forces and internal security: these were the key strategic assets safeguarding the new Kuwait. Education would be the primary means of preparing a new generation of Kuwaitis to be ready and capable of managing the state after independence and to lead the efforts for development. Therefore, he was concerned with education of all types, especially girls' education and physical education, whilst also paying detailed attention to arts and music by encouraging the establishment of art societies: painting, photography, music and performance arts. He was described as the 'patron of arts and music' in Kuwait.

As chairman of the Education Council, Abdullah Mubarak pursued a policy of relentless educational expansion. He pressed for the building of new schools[70] and was concerned with education at all stages: nursery, elementary and secondary.[71] He also succeeded in securing the Emir's support for educational projects, and took pride in telling him of the children's progress. Enlisting the Emir's support was an especially useful means of persuading parents of the value of educating both their sons and daughters.[72] Abdullah Mubarak himself contributed to the development of many projects: for example, he gave an area of 3,248 square metres from his private property, near the Dasman Palace, to build the Health School in 1959.[73]

As a result of these efforts, the number of students increased from 20,500 (15,300 boys and 5,200 girls) in 1954/5 to 35,536 in 1958/9. The number of teachers increased as well, from 1,332 in 1956/7 to 1,697 in 1958/9.[74]

In 1959, Abdullah Mubarak approved an important project to create a proper documentary record of Kuwait's history that would be available to historians and researchers engaged in the study of Kuwait and the history of the Gulf. An appeal was made to all citizens and researchers to participate in preparing the record, by showing any documents or memoirs to the Education Department to ensure their entry into the archival listings.[75]

The Education Council was reformed in 1960 with a wider brief and set of responsibilities. Its first meeting on 29 February was chaired by Sheikh Abdullah Mubarak, who pointed out the significance of the Council's role in 'the education of the younger generation, based on moral principles and loyalty to the homeland'. It was the Council's responsibility to 'supervise' education, which would have a significant impact on the country's future.[76] In its meeting on 7 March the Council discussed the Antiquities Draft Law and the Council's role in preserving and maintaining antiquities, controlling their sale, and developing the concept for a national museum. The project was approved, along with plans to build the first nursery in Failaka island.[77] At a meeting on 14 March, again chaired by Abdullah Mubarak, a report was put forward to build a university: this was not immediately approved – it was agreed to allow more time to study the report in detail.[78]

The Council meetings reveal the growing volume of Kuwait's educational development, including building new schools; expansion of the buildings and services of the existing schools; developing the scout camps; building schools in Sharqa and Ajman Emirates; and educating those with visual, hearing and speech impairment. The Council also planned an institute for those with learning difficulties. For Abdullah Mubarak, this was the essence of a modern state, in which the people were able to develop their human potential to the full. He was always modest about his contribution, however, and diverted attention towards the teachers who had the day-to-day responsibility for education. His contribution was different. When he was young, there had been no such thing as a school like those in the developed world. However, from the 1950s, when he put his energy behind the development of education, the quality of the system began to improve. The success of Kuwaiti students at the highest levels of learning in some of the world's finest universities was a measure of what had been achieved.

§

'Civil society' as described in this chapter was a concept novel to the Arab way of thinking. It usually denotes private and voluntary organizations that perform certain social functions, independent of the state's authority. They include trade unions, scientific societies, chambers of commerce and industry, and public organizations. An active civil society requires the attainment of a certain degree of social maturity, and requires its various groups to organize themselves and to defend their common goals.

Although these societies and institutions generally focus upon a specific social, economic or cultural activity – thus distinguishing them from political parties – their political implications cannot be ignored. Their creation is a means of developing popular participation; they also provide a forum for dialogue and interaction among their members. From the experience of various states, including Kuwait, it is clear that although these societies begin their activities within their specialized functions, they quickly extend them into the political sphere. For this reason, their creation can be an important turning point in the development of any society.

While Sheikh Abdullah Mubarak contributed to the building of the government institutions, he also played a role

Plate 1. A meeting at the Qubba Palace in Cairo after the death of President Gamal Abdel Nasser, with leading political personalities to discuss funeral arrangements and important issues, 29 September 1970. From left to right: Sheikh Abdullah Mubarak, Labib Shuqair (Speaker of the Parliament), Anwar Al-Sadat (Vice-President), Hussein Al-Shafiae (Second Vice-President), Ali Sabri (Secretary General of the Arab Socialist Union), Mahmoud Fowzi (Minister of Foreign Affairs).

Plate 2. Sheikh Abdullah Mubarak in the mid-1940s, surrounded by Sheikh Jaber Ahmed Al-Sabah (to his left, Emir from 1977 to 2006), Sheikh Sabah Ahmed Al-Sabah (on his right, Emir from 2006 to present) and Sulaiman Mousa Al Seif (behind him).

Plate 3. With President Fuad Shehab of Lebanon and King Mohammed V of Morocco on the occasion of Sheikh Abdullah Mubarak being honoured with Lebanon's highest distinction, Beirut 1960.

Plate 4. Sheikh Abdullah Mubarak visiting Kuwaiti students in the United Kingdom and seated next to Mr and Mrs Jackson (responsible for the student office), London, May 1952.

Plate 5. At the Hendon Police College on his first visit to Britain in 1951.

Plate 6. Commemorating the first shipment of oil to be exported from Kuwait with the Emir of Kuwait Sheikh Ahmed Jaber Al-Sabah, 30 June 1946.

Plate 7. Sheikh Abdullah Mubarak at a naval parade in the 1950s.

Plate 8.   Sheikh Abdullah Mubarak being saluted by the Honour
Guards as he exits the headquarters of the Public Security
Department in 1953.

Plate 9. At Kuwait Airport for the first Kuwait Airlines flight, March 1954.

Plate 10. Sheikh Abdullah Mubarak receiving the first class of Kuwaiti pilots after their graduation from the United Kingdom, 1954.

Plate 11. Sheikh Abdullah Mubarak as Commander-in-Chief of the Kuwaiti Armed Forces.

Plate 12. A live ammunition manoeuvre with his officers.

Plate 13. At the official ceremony celebrating the coming to power of Sheikh Abdullah Salem Al-Sabah as Emir of Kuwait, 1950.

Plate 14. Sheikh Abdullah Al Salem and Sheikh Abdullah Mubarak drinking a cup of water at Kuwait's first desalination plant, Shuwaikh, March 1953.

Plate 15. Presidents Gamal Abdel Nasser of Egypt and Choukri Al-Kouatli of Syria visiting Sheikh Abdullah Mubarak at his Alexandria house in 1958. Anwar Al-Sadat and Abdel Hakim Amer appear in the picture.

Plate 16. Sheikh Abdullah Mubarak at his last official function during the visit of King Saud of Saudi Arabia, April 1961.

Plate 17. Sheikh Abdullah Mubarak inspecting the Kuwaiti police force in 1959.

Plate 18. At the wedding of Mona Gamal Abdel Nasser with his wife, Souad Al-Sabah, and first son Mubarak in 1965.

Plate 19. Sheikh Abdullah Mubarak receiving Sheikh Hamad, the Emir of Bahrain, 1958.

Plate 20. Examining the Ahmadi oilfields in 1949 with Abdullah Al-Mulla, Government Secretary (on his right), Sir Phillip Southwell, Managing Director of the Kuwait Oil Company (on his left) and Mr L. T. Jordan, General Manager of the Kuwait Oil Company (behind).

Plate 21. Receiving King Mohammed V of Morocco in 1960.

Plate 22. Receiving Prince Faisal, the Crown Prince of Iraq, in Kuwait, mid-1950s.

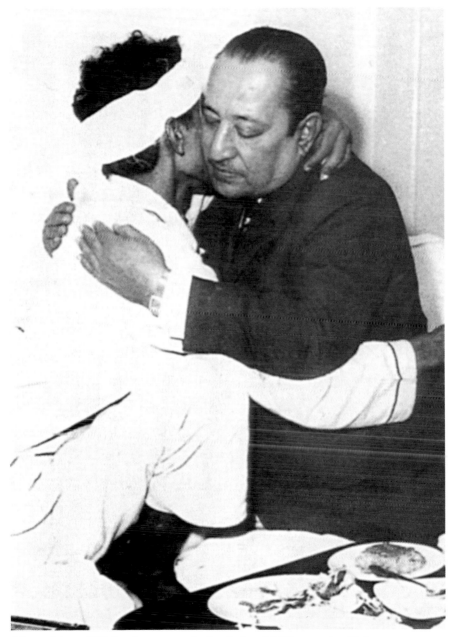

Plate 23. With the wounded of the 1973 war in Cairo.

Plate 24. Taking part in the funereal prayer for the Emir of Kuwait, Sheikh Abdullah Al Salem, 1965.

Plate 25. Commemorative picture of Sheikh Abdullah Mubarak with officers in the mid-1950s.

Plate 26. Official state portrait of the Ruler of Kuwait, Sheikh Abdullah Salem Al-Sabah and the Deputy Ruler, Sheikh Abdullah Mubarak Al-Sabah.

Plate 27. Sheikh Abdullah Mubarak with President Abdulkarim Qassem of Iraq at the opening of the Umm Qasr Port, Iraq, 1960. The Kuwaiti delegation in the second row are Abdulhamid Al-Sane, Nusif Al-Yousef, Hamad Al-Homaizi and Abdulatif Al-Thuwaini.

Plate 28. Visiting President Suleiman Frangieh of Lebanon, Beirut, early 1970s.

Plate 29. Attending a lecture by the Iraqi journalist Mr Yunis Al-Bahri at the Cultural Club in Kuwait. Seated to the left of Sheikh Abdullah Mubarak is Mr Mohamed Salah Al-Din (Egyptian Minister of Foreign Affairs), September 1952.

Plate 30.   With the Syrian leader General Adib Al-Shishakli.

Plate 31. Sheikh Abdullah Mubarak (Head of the Education Council) at the official opening ceremony for the Shuwaikh Secondary School. On his left is Abdulaziz Hussein; while on his right is Sheikh Abdullah Jaber Al-Sabah. In front is Abdulmajeed Mustafa (headmaster).

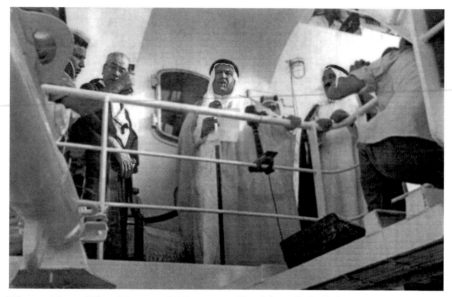

Plate 32. The Emir of Kuwait, Sheikh Abdullah Salem, and his Deputy Ruler, Sheikh Abdullah Mubarak, officially launching Kuwait's first oil tanker *Kazimah*, Ahmadi Port, 1959.

in creating and supporting the non-governmental organizations. In the late 1940s, under the influence of social change and modernization, especially as a result of the country's oil production, Kuwaiti society was in flux. There was a rapid development of new social groupings and institutions that aspired to play a role in public life. For example, educational expansion highlighted students as a social group, and the social 'weight' and status of teachers and graduates increased. Kuwaitis returning from scholarships abroad became more active both socially and intellectually. Such developments had a considerable impact on Kuwaiti society, which is reflected in how the government dealt with the rising aspirations of these groups, not only through appointments in the administrative system but also by opening new channels for expression of opinion and social participation.

Abdullah Mubarak supported the efforts of educated Kuwaiti youth to create social and sports societies. The first attempt was the idea of opening 'Al Nadi Al-Ahli in 1948, but it did not succeed. The idea was then refocused to establish a football team, and the success of the team subsequently led to reconsidering the idea of the club. A founding committee was set up and Abdullah Mubarak was appointed as the club's honorary chairman when it opened in August 1952.[79] At the opening ceremony he declared his appreciation of the role of sport by saying: 'Sport in civilized nations has become a means of spreading virtue and good morals. Sport today is not just for pleasure or amusement, but has become a school for implanting self-confidence and building a new generation with a strong body.'

A month after its opening the club was renamed The National Cultural Club, and newspaper proprietor Younis Al-Bahri was invited to lecture on the 'Arab Cause'. The club also published a monthly magazine called *Al-Iman* (the Faith), which opened its pages to Arab writers who called for the extension of inter-Arab links. During the 1950s, the club played a significant role in the intellectual and cultural life of the country.

Though the law at the time prohibited the club's members from being involved in politics and sectarian matters, the mere existence of the club was an important step towards establishing intellectual clubs in Kuwait and the forming of an institutional framework that allowed the intellectual elite to create dialogue and cultural interaction.

Thus, as this chapter has shown, by the time that Abdullah Mubarak left office in 1961, all the main institutions of a modern society were in place. It was the development of the oil economy after the first exports in 1946 that made change imperative. Abdullah Mubarak served two Rulers with equal loyalty: Sheikh Ahmed al-Jaber Al-Sabah until 1950, and Sheikh Abdullah III al-Salem Al-Sabah (1950–65). It was by the end of Abdullah Mubarak III's period of rule that all the major institutions were in place and functioning effectively. However, this well-functioning state was not built out of nothing in just a few years: it had required sustained action and dedicated leadership over a period of almost two decades. Abdullah Mubarak had provided both, and this sustained work may have been his greatest contribution to changing the lives of every citizen and resident of Kuwait.

~4~

Redefining Kuwait's National Interest

T he central element of Sheikh Abdullah Mubarak's policy for Kuwait's development in the 1950s was redefining the state's national interest. From the British viewpoint, Britain's interest and Kuwait's interest were identical. The experienced and benign British Government in London would set the policy for Kuwait and the Kuwaiti Government would implement it. This applied to both political and economic matters. Sheikh Abdullah Mubarak accepted neither premise. He denied neither the competence nor the efficiency of the British system, but he could not accept the altruism of the British. He believed that Kuwait had to find its own way in the world and, in particular, that it made no sense for Kuwait simply to follow the UK diktat over oil policy. Equally, Kuwait needed to develop its own connection with the United States, rather than allowing the British Government to act as its mouthpiece.

The agreement that Sheikh Mubarak Al-Sabah had signed with the British Government on 23 January 1899 stated that London was to be responsible for the administration of Kuwait's foreign affairs. This covered a wide ground. The agreement further stipulated that no sale, lease, mortgage or occupation of any part of Kuwait to a foreign government or subjects of any other power, for any purpose, could be undertaken without the prior consent of the British Government. Nor should Kuwait receive agents or representatives of any foreign government or power without the prior sanction of the British Government.

Nevertheless, Sheikh Mubarak anticipated the benefit that Kuwait would gain from integrating with the wider world and, accordingly, he developed many international connections. His son Abdullah Mubarak continued along the same path. As early as the 1940s, when very limited flight connections existed between Kuwait and the European cities, Abdullah Mubarak visited a number of Scandinavian states, Switzerland, Greece, France, Italy and Spain as well as the United States and the United Kingdom. This understandably caused direct conflict with the British authorities in Kuwait, who guarded their extensive rights from the 1899 agreement.

The sources of disagreement were concentrated in two principal areas. The first was oil. The British oil companies operating in the Gulf played a dominant role. In the case of Kuwait, for example, Kuwait Oil Company invited many sheikhs to London, arranged their itinerary and determined the people they would meet. It sent analytical reports about these meetings (and other important information) to the Foreign Office. One of the reports addressed to the British Political Resident in the Gulf said that the Foreign Office 'discusses political developments in Kuwait in all frankness with Kuwait Oil Company'[1] – thus making it quite clear the extent to which the oil companies interacted in politics.

The second was the growing rivalry between British and US oil companies, which began to surface as early as the late 1930s.

The United States started to seek special relations with the oil-producing countries with the intention of obtaining exploration concessions for its companies and to find markets for its products. Britain, on the other hand, worked to maintain its traditional role in the Gulf, the role it had exercised alone since the end of the nineteenth century. It tried to maintain its primacy and to counter increasing US pressure, until it conceded in 1968, bowing to the new realities and declaring, on strategic and economic grounds, an 'East of Suez' policy that involved the withdrawal of its military forces from the Gulf region in 1971.

§

Developing relations with the United States

Until the 1940s, the United States covered Kuwaiti affairs from the American Consulate in Basra, whose officials visited Kuwait occasionally to follow the latest developments. US diplomatic reports for this period reveal the near-total dependence of the US on Britain for information. An example is the US Consul's report of 8 February 1950, which requested the Political Agent to arrange a meeting between the consul and Sheikh Abdullah al-Salem. The Political Agent also invited members of the US Consulate in Basra to stay at the Agency's residence during their visit to Kuwait.[2]

The flow of information to the State Department during this period reflected Washington's increased concern with the Gulf region. In a memorandum prepared by the State Department in March 1946 on 'the United States policy towards the Gulf emirates', it stated that: 'While Washington recognizes Britain's special status in the region, our policy stems from the insistence that Britain's special position should not hurt the United

States's interests, or those interests related to the peoples and governments of the region.'[3]

In 1947, the State Department produced a memorandum about Britain's special relations with the states of the region and the policy that the United States should adopt. It offered the view that Britain was the de facto administrator of the foreign policy of the Gulf States. However, this arrangement was not sustainable, as a result of the political and economic developments since 1945. The British withdrew from India in 1947 and their influence in the Gulf correspondingly diminished, at a time when US interests in Saudi Arabia and Bahrain, as well as in Kuwait, were growing. The memorandum concluded: 'For us, it is logical to enquire about the steps which Britain would adopt to recognize this new position in the Gulf and the south of the Arabian Peninsula.'[4]

Establishing a US Consulate in Kuwait became the salient issue in relations between Washington and London during this period. When the idea was first presented in the late 1940s it was obvious that Britain was not eager, though it did not oppose it explicitly. Britain's stand was that despite its appreciation of the US Government's need to open this consulate, London was afraid of the consequences of the decision. Appointing a US Consul in Kuwait would encourage other British-protected states to follow suit.

On 15 April 1948, Britain suggested that the practical solution lay in the US Consulate in Basra offering consular services to Americans in Kuwait through the unofficial appointment of one of its employees as its representative in Kuwait. London also asserted that the representative's contacts with the Ruler of Kuwait and any government entities would still be through the Political Agent.[5] The United States, however, was keen to have independent consular representation in Kuwait. As a consequence of US insistence, the Foreign Office indicated that accepting, in principle, the establishment of a US Consulate in Kuwait, with the sanction of the British Government, it must be with the understanding that the British–Kuwait special relationship and the judicial powers of the Political Agent must be respected. Washington proposed as a compromise that the approval be granted jointly by the British Government and the Ruler of Kuwait, or by the Ruler of Kuwait after obtaining British approval. London refused any of these compromises and refused to change its original position. Finally, the State Department accepted the British conditions based on its legal advisor's recommendation. This decision suggested that the United States was not in a position to dispute the British interpretation of the 1899 agreement, since it was not a party thereto. Moreover, the agreement did not affect any US rights, and if Abdullah Mubarak of Kuwait sided with the British interpretation of the agreement, the Americans would have no case to argue.

This seemed highly unlikely, since several reports to the State Department confirmed Abdullah Mubarak's strong support for opening a US Consulate. He plainly judged that its presence would put pressure on the British and set a limit to their influence. According to the US Consul's last report from Basra on Kuwait, one of his contacts informed him that Abdullah Mubarak of Kuwait was looking forward to the opening of the American Consulate 'to use the American Consul against the British Political Agent'.[6]

Finally, on 12 March 1951, Enoch Duncan became the first American Consul appointed to Kuwait and a consular agreement between the United States and the United Kingdom was signed in Washington on 6 June 1951. Duncan arrived in Kuwait on 27 June, and his first report reflected the nature of the British–American relations and Britain's desire for the Kuwaiti–American relations to pass through the Political Agency. As Duncan indicated in this report, the Political Agent arranged his first meeting with the Ruler of Kuwait on 1 July 1951.

A memorandum prepared by the Division of Near Eastern Affairs in the State Department on 25 March 1952, on the political situation in Kuwait, pointed to two important developments. First, Britain had acted unilaterally and without advance consultation with Washington in a number of issues related to the region's future. Second, there was an obvious trend to expand and support the British hegemony in the region.[7] A US memorandum on Kuwait's legal status and the nature of Britain's relations with it reaffirmed that London's loss of its political positions in India, Iran and Egypt after World War II increased the significance of the Gulf sheikhdoms to the government in London. As a result, Britain was silently shifting the interpretation of Kuwait's legal status from 'being a state with special contractual relations with the UK' to a 'protected state'.[8] This did not concur with Washington's understanding of Kuwait's status.

There were a number of bruising encounters. In 1953, when the issue of transferring the water from Shatt Al-Arab to Kuwait was raised, a British company (Sir Alexander Gibb & Partners) was selected as the consultant. The project documents stipulated that procurement of the major portion of the requirements should be from the 'sterling region'. The US Consul commented by saying these arrangements represented an attempt to exclude American companies from participation in the project.[9] This had already been claimed with respect to oil contracts; nonetheless, Kuwait had successfully made contracts with US oil companies. The same issue resurfaced in 1954 when the

US air attaché in Beirut wrote to the State Department on the circumstances surrounding the strongly contested establishment of Kuwait Airways Company: Abdullah Mubarak took one view and the Political Agency another. The attaché urged Washington to step in, with the aim of finding a role for the American companies either in the management or in the purchase of aircraft. If negotiations with Britain failed, the report said that the Kuwaitis would be in need of foreign assistance, and Washington should be ready to intervene.[10]

The British–American rivalry over oil had begun in the early 1930s, and US diplomatic reports illustrate the strenuous efforts it made to acquire oil exploration concessions.[11] Yet Britain was determined to use its special position in Kuwait for the exclusive benefit of the British oil companies. Therefore, it stipulated that companies seeking concessions should be registered in England and that any concession by the Ruler of Kuwait should contain a British control clause. In response, Washington accused London of breaching the open-door policy, and that it had ensured that the Anglo-Persian Oil Company obtain the concession instead of the Eastern General Group Ltd, which was backed by the USA.

Faced with increasing US pressure, London accepted the argument and dropped the British control clause. The Foreign Office then agreed to establish the Kuwait Oil Company (KOC) as a partnership between the Anglo-Persian Oil Company and the American Gulf Company. The company was to be registered in London as a British firm, the British share should not be less than 50 per cent of the capital, and the company representatives' contacts with the Kuwaiti authorities should be through the Political Agent.[12]

However, this did not set a binding precedent. The conflict surfaced again in June 1948; the State Department notified its embassy in London that it accepted the approval of Kuwait's Ruler to grant an American company an exploration licence in the Neutral Zone with Saudi Arabia, subject to the British Government's approval. Britain privately believed that the licence would never be granted as the Saudi approval for working in the Neutral Zone would be withheld.[13] The State Department instructed the embassy to intervene with the British authorities so as to reach a compromise among all the parties. The Kuwaitis favoured the US bid and in July 1948 the matter was settled, with the American Independent Oil Company (Aminoil) obtaining the concession. According to one report, Aminoil's oil exploration activity in the Neutral Zone was a source for British alarm.[14]

The role of the Kuwait Oil Company

As we have seen, the Kuwait Oil Company (KOC) was a joint venture between a British and a US oil company. Abdullah Mubarak's visit to the United States stemmed from a meeting on 20 March 1952 with Colonel Drake, KOC's chairman and his deputy, Hamilton. At this meeting, the idea of a visit was proposed and fully discussed for the first time, with Abdullah Mubarak making clear his strong desire to visit the United States. When Drake and Hamilton returned to Washington, they submitted a report about Kuwait to the State Department, with the prospect of building a good understanding with Abdullah Mubarak. They proposed an official invitation to the USA, which the State Department warmly endorsed, promising all necessary assistance to ensuring its success. Abdullah Mubarak received the invitation on 20 April.

On the next day, he informed the US Consul that his travel plans depended on the Ruler's schedule during the summer, and whether the Ruler's absence would require his presence in Kuwait. In a cable dated 25 April, the consul stated that he expected the visit would take place,[15] and he confirmed this in another cable dated 9 June. Although KOC's office in London did not receive any response or confirmation from Abdullah Mubarak about the exact dates of his visit, its employees booked him aboard the Cunard liner *Queen Mary*. In mid-June 1952, Abdullah Mubarak arrived in London and KOC's representative was under the impression that he was en route to Washington, but a few days later he told them he could not proceed with the plan. What 'could not' meant in these circumstances was clarified by US diplomatic sources in London: the reports to Washington indicated that Britain had suggested he should decline the invitation, but had promised in return that his request for the arms needed for the Kuwaiti Army would be met by British companies. The inference is that had Abdullah Mubarak visited the USA, after American companies had secured a major role in oil exploration and production, the possibility was that he would naturally turn to the USA for defence supplies and other needs. The Foreign Office démarche was to prevent any further loosening of the connection with Britain.

According to the US Consul in Kuwait, the motive behind the British stance was fear that friendly relations between members of the ruling family and the United States might develop.[16] Such a relationship could undermine Britain's aim that any contacts between Kuwait and the world should continue to be through London. This fear was based on the aftermath of Sheikh Fahad Al-Salem's visit to the United States in 1951. He made clear his feeling that the United States was more advanced than England and Europe and, according to the British Political Agent, this had a negative impact on his view of Britain.[17]

Following Sheikh Fahad Al-Salem's honest but impolitic declaration, Sheikh Abdullah Mubarak's visit to the United States became still more of a delicate matter. Would he exacerbate the bruised feelings already created, or could he find a way to resolve the difficulty and at the same time advance Kuwaiti interests? An indication of the high issues at stake was that Abdullah Mubarak's secretary, Ezzat Jaafar, refused to translate a question by J. M. Cooper, KOC's deputy chairman, concerning the visit to the United States. It could not be discussed, he said, because of the sensitivity of the issue for Abdullah Mubarak. The matter was concluded on 22 June, when he left London for Paris – the visit to the United States did not happen.

Although the British documents do not contain any reference to the Foreign Office raising the issue of the visit with Sheikh Abdullah Mubarak, it was certainly believed at the time that the cancellation came as a direct response to Britain's wishes. The director of the Eastern Department at the Foreign Office wrote to the Political Agent in Kuwait that news about the intervention in the visit was 'baseless'. 'We do not', he averred, 'have any justification for interference', thus claiming that the decision to cancel the visit belonged to Abdullah Mubarak alone: 'Abdullah Mubarak should not feel he did that to please us.'[18] This was the official story, as far as London was concerned. Abdullah Mubarak was naturally pleased with the outcome: he had broken the dogged British resistance to supplying the Kuwaiti Army, and it was still open to him to develop a warm relationship with the USA at a later date.

The relationship with the United States blossomed, although Kuwait and the United States had divergent views on the threat of communism in the region. Commercial ties grew, but without raising opposition in London. It is clear that collaboration became the norm. When, in 1956, the Ruler's special secretary and Sheikh Abdullah Mubarak's close aide, Bader Abdullah Al-Mulla, visited the US Consulate in Kuwait on 6 October 1956 and requested assistance in obtaining information about the armoured personnel carriers made in the USA, they were warmly welcomed. The Kuwaiti Army had a pressing need for these vehicles for transporting troops and Kuwait wanted to import the vehicles from the USA.

Behind the request stood Sheikh Abdullah Mubarak, who strongly wanted the deal to be completed.[19] He knew that the American equipment was far superior to anything on offer from Britain, and he saw that this was the ideal opportunity to open supply channels with the United States. In October 1958, his deputy in the army command made an additional enquiry for military amphibious vehicles. The consulate reacted quickly, passing over a list of the manufacturers of the vehicles. Simultaneously, the consul asked the State Department to negotiate with the Department of Defense on supplying the Kuwaiti Army with this new equipment.

Abdullah Mubarak was also keen to know how the US would react to any foreign attack on Kuwait and to what extent it would be prepared to defend the country.[20] Moreover, he wanted to discover the degree of British–American coordination over Gulf security. Therefore, in the British–Kuwaiti talks about security issues in the Gulf region, Washington agreed that the British delegation should inform the Deputy Ruler that the British plans for defending Kuwait were discussed in some detail by the United States within the framework of continued coordination between the two countries in defence matters related to the region. However, that did not mean an American commitment to defend Kuwait.[21] Washington also wanted to know more details about military cooperation plans between

Kuwait and Britain, especially those related to building a military base at Al-Dhabaiya and the prospect of stockpiling weapons in Kuwait.[22]

It seems that the roots of British–US coordination in respect of Kuwait date back to the late 1940s. A memorandum by the State Department in 1947 indicated that Britain had informed the USA of its plans to build an important military base in Kuwait. The British further stated that, despite the Saudi–Iraqi conflicts, the project could be implemented by cooperation with Iraq without significant Saudi opposition.[23]

In a report to the Secretary of State in 1959 regarding the attitude of the USA towards a possible Iraqi aggression on Kuwait, the opinion was that should Kuwait ask for military assistance from the United States, this assistance would be granted within the framework of the Middle East Resolution approved by Congress on 9 March 1957 (known as the Eisenhower Plan). Its second paragraph stated the following:

> The United States considers preserving the independence of the Middle East countries vital to its national security and world peace. To achieve that objective, and subject to the President's determination of the necessity situation, the United States shall be ready to use its military force to assist any state or a group of states requesting assistance against any military aggression from any state controlled by international communism, provided this usage be in accord with the contracted commitments and the Constitution of the United States of America.

The report makes it clear that using military force is subject to two conditions:

1) The state should be exposed to aggression and should request assistance.
2) The aggression should come from a state under the control of international communism.

The report added that these two conditions applied to Iraq and that the Kuwaiti Government's request for assistance was a necessary condition – a request from the United Kingdom was not sufficient. If the request for US intervention came from London alone, the US position would be weak from a legal perspective. If the Kuwaiti Government objected, that would be a serious impediment.[24]

It is worth mentioning that during this period the prospect of Kuwait obtaining arms from the United States was considered under the Mutual Security Act. When the State Department discussed the subject, Kuwait's legal status was raised and whether or not it was considered to be under British protection. If it was, providing it with weapons did not require any special measures, due to Britain's responsibility for the good use of weapons. The State Department's legal advisor took the view that the existing relationship between Kuwait and Britain did not provide London with the ability to control or monitor defence matters and it did not control the army in Kuwait. Consequently, Britain was not in a position to guarantee Kuwait's compliance with the rules of using American weapons in accordance with the Mutual Security Act. The legal advisor concluded by saying that supplying Kuwait with arms needed special approval from the US president.[25]

Relations with the United Kingdom

The UK remained the dominant power in the Gulf region and the protector of Kuwait. As a result, the Political Resident in the Gulf and the Political Agent in Kuwait played important roles in the region. In this context, the complex interplay between Kuwaiti interests and British interests made Abdullah Mubarak's relations with Britain extremely intricate. London was aware of his power and influence in Kuwait, his immovable determination, his pride and his dignity. This led them to two apparently contradictory conclusions. First, that he was a committed and responsible person, the safety valve of Kuwait, and possessed the power to maintain internal stability. Yet, second, that he could not be trusted because of his independence of mind and self-confidence – the very qualities that made him the safety valve of Kuwait and increased his domestic influence.

London was permanently uneasy, for example, about his friendship with Gamal Abdul Nasser and his support for the Algerian revolution. It was deeply suspicious of the initiatives he undertook without prior consultation with the Political Agent. There were many examples. One was the waiving of entry visas for Arabs; another was accepting a decoration from the Lebanese Government in 1949 before he had received permission from His Majesty's Government. This was partly due to the interminable delays that the British Government imposed before coming to a decision. Impulsive by nature, Abdullah Mubarak's snap judgements were often based on a highly attuned sense of making the right move at the right time. A decisive gesture such as accepting the Lebanese honour would become a discourtesy if delayed for six months or more while Kuwait waited for the cumbersome British process to grind through its stages.

The process could be most positively described as *sedate*. For example, the Political Agent sent a report to the British Resident seeking advice[26] – and one month's pause for mature consideration followed. In his comment on the subject, the Political Agent referred to a precedent involving the Ruler of Kuwait, Sheikh Ahmed al-Jaber, who had asked the British authorities whether on official occasions he could wear the 'Al-Radifain' decoration given to him by Iraq in 1932: this request merited detailed consideration and interdepartmental consideration by the government in London, who eventually agreed and said it did not object to accepting awards from foreign states but that this must only take place after informing London.[27]

The imputation was that Abdullah Mubarak's contacts with other Arab rulers, ministers or even private citizens were fraught with menace to British interests. A report by the Political Agent in August 1955 stated that Sheikh Abdullah Mubarak had representatives in Lebanon and perhaps in Cairo and that it was likely he would begin repudiating British control of Kuwait's foreign relations. No evidence was offered for this conclusion.[28]

The waiving of entry visas for Arabs into Kuwait might legitimately have been deemed an internal matter. Abdullah Mubarak differed with the British over the naturalization of Arabs. He issued Kuwaiti passports to a large number of Arabs living in Kuwait. When the Political Agent raised this issue after an Iraqi obtained a Kuwaiti passport, Sheikh Abdullah Mubarak answered that issuing passports to Arabs working in Kuwait was a domestic matter. He might have added that Scots did not require a visa to enter England. The Political Agent contacted the Ruler of Kuwait and asked him to issue instructions that passports should not be provided for non-Kuwaitis,[29] which according to US Consular reports to Washington gave rise to Abdullah Mubarak's immediate objection to the intervention into Kuwait's domestic affairs.[30]

It was not only Abdullah Mubarak who was criticized for his pan-Arab beliefs. In 1958, the Political Agent arraigned Abdul Aziz Hussein, director of education, for his pro-Egyptian views and the issuing of contracts to Egyptian teachers. Britain did not welcome this expansion as it saw the teachers as insidious vehicles for spreading anti-Western ideologies. Abdullah Mubarak, informed of the high-handed British demands for a change in policy, denounced the attitude and behaviour of the Political Agent, deeming it a violation of Kuwait's sovereignty.[31] The British documents are full of reports and telegrams from the Political Agent warning his government against the grim consequences of the Kuwaiti Army purchasing arms that would enhance Sheikh Abdullah Mubarak's position vis-à-vis other sheikhs and strengthen his position within the ruling family. It would also 'increase the difficulty of dealing with him'.[32]

Other reports reflected the fear that Abdullah Mubarak might become the Ruler of Kuwait (this will be further explored in Chapter 6). These British anxieties grew from Abdullah Mubarak's forthright criticism of the British. In April 1956, an Agency report recounted that during one of his visits to Beirut he had lunch with some British nationals at Emile Al-Bustani's house. When he left, he upbraided Al-Bustani for inviting him to a meal with those 'British dogs' and declared that he intended to have them out of Kuwait before long.[33] In another report by the British Embassy in Beirut in 1958, it stated that when Paulus Farah, the deputy ruler of Lebanon, warned him that his statements in Cairo would be interpreted as anti-British, Abdullah Mubarak responded in anger by saying that it was none of his business and that 'he would teach those British bastards a lesson and crush their head under his foot'.[34] Undoubtedly, Abdullah

Mubarak was known to have a short fuse, and was unafraid to retaliate in an argument. Yet this kind of rhetorical hyperbole was exceptional.

Sheikh Abdullah Mubarak made numerous visits to Britain, which he enjoyed enormously. The British Government hoped these vists would deepen his admiration of Britain's economic progress. British officials used to extend the visit by many days, during which he could carry out the officially prepared programme[35] – unsurprisingly, he was always keen to review the programme of visits before accepting the invitation. He was also very careful that any invitation was an official one from Her Majesty's Goverment rather than from the oil company.[36] One of his visits to Britain took place in late May 1956 at the invitation of General Gerald Templer, the chief of the Imperial General Staff, which included a visit to Scotland Yard, Hampton Court and the Southbank Centre in London. He also visited Windsor Castle, the Houses of Parliament, the BBC TV building and the Royal Academy of Arts. He met Foreign Secretary Selwyn Lloyd,[37] and was keen to meet Kuwaiti students at universities in the UK.

The 1958 revolution in Iraq and the alliance of Qassem's regime with the Soviet Union transformed the relationship with Britain. The Iraqi threat to Kuwait increased, and the leaders of Kuwait felt the necessity of adopting additional steps to secure the country. Suddenly, Abdullah Mubarak, according to a British report, expressed his country's desire to have joint military planning with Britain. The British evaluation was that the developments in Iraq that had led to the Kuwaitis' increased anxiety would make them more amenable. In this situation, London might seize the opportunity to develop bilateral military cooperation. In the report by the Political Resident to the Foreign Office on 25 April 1959, he mentioned that the foreign danger forced Abdullah Mubarak to co-operate with Britain.[38]

Equally, the Iraqi revolution caused a major change in British strategic thinking and increased British interest in Kuwait's security and the approach to defence. This change in London stemmed from the belief that the relationship that linked London with the old regime in Baghdad allowed Britain to influence Iraq's stance towards Kuwait. The assumption of power by the military might encourage Iraq to be more aggressive towards Kuwait. Therefore, the British military leaders were in sympathy with Abdullah Mubarak in his effort to enhance the military capabilities of his country. They developed a plan for military intervention in Kuwait, coded 'Vantage',[39] in the event of foreign aggression.

Abdullah Mubarak recognized the significance of military cooperation with Britain as a deterrent to Iraqi ambitions in Kuwait. He was keen to keep this cooperation, but within limits and in proportion to Kuwait's interests. Therefore, he was not enthusiastic about the idea of British forces being sent to Kuwait as a precautionary measure against disturbance, and confirmed to the Political Agent the capability of his forces to protect the airport and the Ahmadi port until the arrival of the British forces.[40]

When the British Resident Sir Bernard Burrows questioned the loyalty of the Iraqi elements in Kuwait's security forces, Abdullah Mubarak assured him of his confidence in the forces, and that the loyalty of non-Kuwaiti elements was regularly monitored.[41] Yet it seemed that the British authorities did not find Abdullah Mubarak's assurance sufficient on its own. A report by the US Consul in Kuwait entitled 'The general temper in Kuwait three weeks after the Iraqi revolution', dated 4 August 1958, said that the Political Agent had expressed that he was not entirely confident of the accuracy of those assurances.[42]

Against this background, Sheikh Abdullah Mubarak sought to develop military cooperation with Britain.[43] He sent a number of officers for training with British forces in Bahrain and asked the Political Resident to establish a permanent wireless communication line between the Kuwaiti Army and the British forces in Bahrain.[44] He also approved the stockpiling of weapons[45] and ammunition to be used in any emergency by the British forces (some reports cited the Al-Dhabaiya area in southern Kuwait as the location for stockpiling arms).[46]

On 19 June 1959, the American Embassy in London sent a report to the State Department informing it of Britain's final decision on the stationing of military equipment and ammunition in Kuwait for use in an emergency. On the same day, a British military mission arrived from Bahrain to discuss the issue with Sheikh Abdullah Mubarak, who was at the time acting as Deputy Ruler, and an agreement on details was reached. He requested a reduction in the number of maintenance technicians, and Kuwait pledged to train Kuwaiti technicians to undertake that task. Orders were issued to the British forces command in Aden to prepare the necessary plans to implement the agreement.[47]

Abdullah Mubarak set in motion plans to increase the size of the Kuwaiti Army to 3,000. He accepted in principle the appointment of a British expert in the Public Security Department to support Kuwait in detecting any hostile activity or in case of intelligence reports of any threat.[48] In May 1959, Sheikh Abdullah Mubarak visited Brigadier Tinker, commander of the British Army in Bahrain. He took the opportunity to find out the types of tanks and bombers that Britain had sent to

Iraq before the revolution. He also met with commanders of British forces in Kenya and Aden.[49]

To secure Kuwait against any future foreign aggression, Abdullah Mubarak also needed to be fully aware of current US thinking. In a meeting with the US Consul in Kuwait he was told that in the summit conference between Harold Macmillan and the American president Dwight Eisenhower in 1959, they had exchanged information about the British–American plan for defending Kuwait against any probable Iraqi moves.[50] These efforts led to an agreement with Britain for the defence of Kuwait in the event of a foreign attack. The letter sent by the commander of the British forces in Arabia, dated 12 May 1960, reflected the detailed content of this bilateral agreement.

What do these events and incidents signify about Sheikh Abdullah Mubarak's role in Kuwait's foreign policy? In all of them, he acted from a deep understanding of Kuwait's position in both local and international terms, and also an acceptance of Kuwait's situation and the limitations constraining small states in the international arena. He was also realistic in his political dealings, realizing that Kuwait's influence at times could be enhanced through the interplay of larger, competing Western states. Broadly based foreign relations were, he realized, a necessity for the survival and growth of small states, a guarantee for their existence and independence.

To develop and diversify Kuwait's foreign relations, with a view to Kuwait not depending solely on a single ally, was high on his agenda. He had no hesitation in developing a stronger relationship with the United States as a means to putting pressure on Britain, always taking care to make sure that Washington was informed of the discussions between Kuwait and London regarding security issues in the region and protecting Kuwait from foreign threats.

At the regional level, Abdullah Mubarak strengthened Kuwait's relations with a large number of Arab states. To him, inter-Arab relations were not a foreign policy issue; he dealt with the Arab network of states as one of affiliation and common culture. He considered Kuwait as part of the Arab struggle for liberation, independence, development and reconstruction. As such he strongly supported the armament of the Egyptian, Syrian and Jordanian armies.

For this reason, he also steadfastly supported the struggle of the Algerian and Palestinian peoples. At the same time, his stance towards the Western-centred Baghdad Pact and the Hashemite Union was unenthusiastic; he saw greater value in supporting more solid Arab causes such as Egyptian–Syrian unity and, even more important, Kuwait's joining the Arab League. All these activities and initiatives were centred on what would be necessary to support and protect a fully independent Kuwait. Abdullah Mubarak knew that regional and international support would be fundamental to Kuwait's further development, or even survival itself. When Abdul Karim Qassem objected to Kuwait's independence in 1961, Kuwait managed to mobilize Arab and international support on a wide front. This display of support returned when Iraq, led by Saddam Hussein, finally invaded Kuwait in 1990.

~5~

The Challenge of Iraq

Iraq was a central focus throughout Abdullah Mubarak's political career, and even extending into the period beyond his resignation until the end of his life. As a powerful, aggressive and unreliable neighbour Iraq was a constant source of anxiety. It began under his father's rule, during the first years of modern Kuwait. The Ottomans had always claimed suzerain authority over Kuwait, as part of Turkish Mesopotamia. In practice, this meant very little and Kuwait enjoyed a considerable degree of autonomy. After the collapse of the Ottoman Empire in 1918, the successor state – Iraq – inherited that claim to suzerainty. In reality, the two states, Iraq and Kuwait, had a great deal in common. Their two deserts overlapped; the human and commercial contacts between the two countries were continuous. However, while the problems with Kuwait's other large neighbour – the Saudi kingdom – were diminishing, political difficulties with Iraq grew inexorably. Yet, despite this antagonism, Kuwaitis always had close ties with Iraq, often through marriage and properties held there; an important part of Sheikh Mubarak Al-Sabah's estate lay within Iraq in the region of Al-Faw.

Like his father, Abdullah Mubarak understood Iraq extremely well. With his long-term responsibility for security and combating smuggling, he had developed close relations with the people of Basra and southern Iraq. On an official level, he was a close friend to many Iraqi politicians and army officers. The president of Iraq, Abdul-Salam Aref, visiting Egypt in 1965 met with President Nasser and Abdullah Mubarak. Nasser asked Aref about Iraq and he answered: 'Why do you ask me while you have Abu *Najm* [Abdullah Mubarak] with you?' He added that Sheikh Abdullah Mubarak knew the majority of politicians and army officers in Iraq and that he had known the Sheikh since he was a junior army officer, when he escorted Abdullah Mubarak on a number of his visits to Iraq in the 1950s.

Relations between the two states were, however, marred by Iraq's pursuit of its economic and political demands upon Kuwait, the origins of which lay far back in the Ottoman period. This became more pressing as Kuwait grew increasingly prosperous. The areas of potential conflict lay in Iraq's ambitions in the Gulf. This included the aim to build a new port at Umm Qasr, bordering Kuwait's territory across a narrow strip of water. Iraq wanted to make Kuwait's supply of fresh water from Shatt Al-Arab conditional on obtaining the strategic Warba island. Iraq would only accept a formal demarcation of borders on its own terms, which would mean Kuwait losing territory. The underlying objective was hegemony over Kuwait and, from the 1940s, access to its oil resources. Successive rulers in Baghdad used a variety of legal and political arguments to bring Kuwait under their control, culminating in the military invasion of Kuwait on 2 August 1990.

The border issue was one that rulers of Iraq and Kuwait sought repeatedly to resolve, but without success. The bilateral traditional boundaries had been defined in the agreement concluded between the Ottoman state and Britain on 29 July 1913, by which the two parties acknowledged that Kuwait's territory formed a self-governing (autonomous) district (*caza*) within the Ottoman Empire. However, this document was never ratified because the Ottoman Empire declared war on Britain in 1914. During the period between 1920 and 1923, negotiations continued between Iraq and Kuwait under British supervision; again London reaffirmed the terms of the 1913 Convention – at that time, Britain controlled Iraq under a League of Nations mandate.

Iraqi–Kuwaiti relations entered a new phase with Iraq's independence in 1932. For the purposes of obtaining membership of the League of Nations, Iraq was required to define its borders, including the Iraqi–Kuwaiti frontier. In July 1932, the British High Commissioner in Baghdad and the Iraqi Acting Prime Minister Ja'afar Al-Askari, and later Prime Minister Nouri As-Sa'eed, exchanged letters. By September they had reached agreement. At that point the Emir of Kuwait, Sheikh Ahmed al-Jaber, visited Iraq and met King Faisal I who accorded him the 'Al-Rafidein decoration', the highest Iraqi order.[1]

However, when King Ghazi Al-Faisal succeeded his father in 1933 he immediately opened a new campaign against Kuwait. Sheikh Ahmed al-Jaber tried to deal with the situation by visiting Iraq in 1935 and meeting the King. But no solution could be found. The Emir visited Iraq again later in the same year and raised the issue once more with King Ghazi. Again, the discussions ended in stalemate. Then, in 1936, Iraqi Prime Minister Nouri As-Sa'eed tried a different angle of approach. He talked to the British Ambassador in Baghdad, saying that Basra was unsuitable as Iraq's main port and it was imperative that an agreement should be reached with Kuwait to obtain another outlet onto the Gulf. He added, with a menacing undertone, 'I, as an Arab, hope to see Kuwait integrated peacefully with Iraq as the Emirate cannot withstand the armed forces of Iraq.'[2]

Iraq applied fresh pressure on Kuwait, and the situation deteriorated further in 1938 when Baghdad began to call publicly for Kuwait's annexation. At the beginning of the year, King Ghazi set up a special radio station at the Al-Zuhur Palace in Baghdad to broadcast propaganda in support of Iraqi claims to Kuwait. In March 1938, the Iraqi Foreign Minister announced that the appropriate solution, from the Iraqi point of view, was to have an Iraqi port on the sea.[3] In August, the Iraqi cabinet sent Foreign Minister Tawfiq Al-Suweidi to the League of Nations in Geneva, and also to Paris and London, to discuss a number of pressing matters, including Iraq's relations with Kuwait.[4]

Some interpreted Iraq's intensified campaign at that time as a direct result of relinquishing a major portion of its sovereignty over Shatt Al-Arab to Iran, in accordance with the 1937 agreement between the two countries. It was also a consequence of the oil discoveries in the Kuwaiti Burgan area, which Iraq thought might help to solve its economic problems. In March 1939, there were more calls for the use of military force against Kuwait. However, the British authorities moved five divisions of the British Army in Iraq to the border, forcing Iraq to retreat.

The situation changed when King Ghazi died in a mysterious motor accident in April 1939, leaving his three-year-old son as his heir. Foul play was widely suspected and the internal politics of Iraq lurched into public disorder. In 1941, the British ousted the pro-Axis Prime Minister Rashid Ali, taking control of Iraq for the duration of World War II.

The end of World War II produced no better relationship between Kuwait and Iraq. In Kuwait, Sheikh Ahmed al-Jaber was alarmed by a fresh wave of riots in Baghdad during 1948 and by the dangerous uncertainty that continued thereafter. From a Kuwaiti point of view, a settlement of the frontier issue was even more essential than before. Without an agreement, there was no way of creating a stable base for the future. On 10 January 1950 the Emir, three days prior to his death, sent a letter to the Political Agent requesting the intervention of the British Government to demarcate the borders. The British Resident in the Gulf, Sir Robert Hay, sent a report to the Foreign Office pointing to the seriousness of the issue, and wondering if it 'was possible to start setting up a committee to discuss common borders'.[5]

All through the early 1950s, Kuwait initiated attempt after attempt to reach a final solution to the border problem. In early 1951, the question of boundary demarcation was raised again. Iraq said it was ready to participate if Kuwait agreed to include Warba island within Iraq's borders, claiming it was essential for the protection of Umm Qasr port, which Iraq intended to build. In March 1952, Sheikh Abdullah Al-Salem visited Iraq at the invitation of Prince Abdul-Ilah, the Regent for King Ghazi's young son, Faisal II. During the Emir's visit, Iraq reaffirmed the precondition of Kuwait relinquishing Warba, before any demarcation of the borders.

At the end of the same month, Crown Prince Faisal visited Kuwait, accompanied by senior officials, including the Regent, Prince Abdul-Ilah, his grandmother Queen Nafisa, Prime Minister Jamil Al-Madfa'i and Defence Minister Nouri As-Sa'eed. As the Emir was in Europe, Sheikh Abdullah Mubarak greeted the delegation.

The next month, April 1952, Sheikh Abdullah Mubarak returned the compliment by making an official visit to Iraq. In May 1953, he was the head of the Kuwaiti delegation to King Faisal II's coronation, which was attended by representatives from 32 states.[6] In 1954, he visited Iraq again and held talks with Iraqi Acting Foreign Minister Shaker Al-Wadi. They agreed to hold direct negotiations in the future to address common issues, including the borders.[7] However, Iraq maintained its long-standing claim to Warba island and a 4-kilometre-wide strip along Al-Sabiya Khor, south of the border, to enable Iraq to develop Umm Qasr port.[8] The negotiations were terminated. In October 1955, Prime Minister Nouri As-Sa'eed returned to the topic in a telephone conversation with the British Ambassador in Baghdad, stressing once more the primary importance of developing Umm Qasr port for Iraq, as an outlet for exporting oil and as an alternative to the port of Basra. In December of the same year, he suggested a 99-year lease of the Kuwaiti land necessary for the project. Kuwaiti efforts to reach a solution continued, with Sheikh Abdullah Mubarak visiting Iraq in October 1957[9] and again in May 1958, and for a third time in October 1958.[10] All these efforts and contacts yielded nothing.[11]

Iraq's efforts to bring Kuwait under its influence were unrelenting throughout this period. In 1953, Iraqi Prime Minister Fadel Al-Jamali had suggested to the British Ambassador in Baghdad that 'The real solution to Kuwait's problem was its annexation by Iraq'.[12] In 1954, the Iraqi Foreign Minister had informed the British Ambassador in Baghdad, and the Political Resident in Bahrain, that 'Iraq does not really recognize Kuwait's Independence'.[13] In 1955, Iraq tried to include Kuwait in the Baghdad Pact but failed. Given the increased importance of Iraq from a Western strategic perspective, Nouri As-Sa'eed imagined that he could neutralize the British role in Iraq's relationship with Kuwait. He escalated his demands; instead of demanding a lease on the land necessary for developing Umm Qasr port, he demanded border changes that would bring these areas under Iraqi sovereignty. Kuwaiti apprehension soared.

Water supply as a bargaining point

The water problem in Kuwait stemmed from the fact that a major portion of its drinkable water came from Shatt Al-Arab, carried in ships from Iraq to Kuwait. The Kuwait Water Company was set up in 1939, with a large fleet of ships that carried water from Shatt Al-Arab and unloaded it into tanks built in Kuwait Bay. Unfortunately, the creation of the company created more problems than it solved as the system of storage did not meet the necessary public health requirements; moreover, water supplies were frequently delayed or halted for extended periods.[14]

In 1936, the Ruler of Kuwait, Sheikh Ahmed al-Jaber, had suggested to the British authorities that building a pipeline from Shatt Al-Arab to Kuwait would secure the necessary volume of water for drinking and agriculture. At that time, the Iraqi Government welcomed the idea, but Britain was not enthusiastic. In the early 1950s the project was revived. The Iraqi Government agreed initially, but political obstacles soon emerged. In May 1952, Iraq repeated its desire to acquire Warba island and its opposite coast to build an Iraqi port at Umm Qasr. The Iraqi Oil Company proposed a project to build a pipeline to carry the Iraqi oil from Al-Zubair, from the Basra oilfield to the sea near Al-Ahmadi port. Iraq reiterated its demands in 1954.

The American Consul in Kuwait wrote on 23 January 1956, that after one year of negotiations with Iraq the Kuwaiti Government had decided not to go ahead with the water pipeline project. The report gave several explanations for Kuwait's decision, including Kuwaiti reluctance to depend for its drinking water on a single source controlled by another state. Anti-Western and pro-Egyptian feelings might have contributed to the decision as well. Kuwait had no wish to become embroiled in the Arab cold war between Cairo and Baghdad, or to adopt a position against the Egyptian, Syrian and Saudi coalition.[15] Some Iraqi officials explained Kuwait's decision as a consequence of Saudi pressure on Kuwait. This was certainly the opinion of Hikmat Al-Jaderji, director of Arab affairs at the Iraqi Ministry of Foreign Affairs, in a telephone conversation with the American Embassy in Baghdad.[16] However, the Kuwaiti decision was motivated by a clear understanding of the risks inherent in any closer connection with an aggressively expansionist Iraq.

Kuwait's decision wrong-footed the Iraqi Government. Iraqi Foreign Minister Burhan-El-Dinn Pash Ayan was quick to issue a statement denying Iraq's demand for amending the existing borders as a precondition for approving the water pipeline.[17] But in reality, Iraq continued to link the water pipeline to the border question. Sheikh Abdullah Mubarak completely rejected Iraq's demands. He single-mindedly emphasized Kuwait's independence and sovereignty over its territories and resources. Therefore, when the Iraqi Foreign Minister sent an encouraging letter to the Emir of Kuwait, Sheikh Abdullah Al-Salem, in April 1956, Abdullah Mubarak replied on the Emir's behalf thanking Iraq for its warm sentiments and stating that it was 'what he always expected from our Iraqi brothers'.[18] He stressed Kuwait's readiness to negotiate with Iraq on the border issue, on the basis of the letters exchanged in 1932 between Iraqi Prime Minister Nouri As-Sa'eed and the British Political Agent. However, he refused to link an agreement with the border issue, or to share oil revenues. He also affirmed Kuwait's need for its oil revenue. This was no different from Kuwait's need for water, or Iraq's desire for a pipeline to transport its own oil.

According to the report of the American Consul in Kuwait on 11 March 1957, the Supreme Council had discussed the project presented by Iraq in early February and recommended the Ruler to approve neither the water pipeline project nor the oil pipeline proposed by the Iraqi Oil Company, until the border issue was settled. The US Consulate recommended that several steps should be taken to improve Iraqi–Kuwaiti relations because these would best serve Western interests in the region. It also recommended that the State Department should press Baghdad to accept the Kuwaiti position. In light of the letters exchanged in 1932,[19] it was clear that a settlement of the borders was still possible. Britain also suggested a compromise, calling for demarcation of the border at the points where water pipelines crossed the frontier. The Emir of Kuwait and his deputy, Abdullah Mubarak, refused a partial solution that ignored the larger boundary dispute.[20]

King Faisal of Iraq invited Sheikh Abdullah Mubarak to visit Baghdad during Eid Al-Fitr in order to convince him that Iraq had no territorial ambitions in Kuwait. But that did not change anything. Kuwait had now adopted a fundamentally different approach to the water supply problem: desalination of sea water. Indeed, the largest distillation and desalination plant in the whole world was built in Kuwait in 1958, with a capacity of 2 million gallons per day.

In a press interview after the Iraqi revolution of July 1958, Sheikh Abdullah Mubarak answered a question about the negotiations with the old regime for conveying Shatt Al-Arab water to Kuwait. He said:

> There were negotiations, but they also wanted to alienate us from our neutrality ... where we live as friends with the entire world and as brothers to all Arabs everywhere, opening our homes and industrial and commercial establishments, our schools and government departments for every Arab to work, in dignity and with pride. The leaders of the old Iraqi [Hashemite] regime proposed unity with Iraq in return for supplying us with drinking water from Shatt Al-Arab. I answered with the loudest voice: 'We shall never relinquish one foot of our lands even if we die of thirst'. Then they said 'Let us share in the oil revenues'. I answered them: 'Never; these revenues are the property of the Kuwaiti people, allocated for reform projects and construction'. They reiterated the offer directly and indirectly and I reiterated my rejection with determination until they despaired and realized that Kuwait was the Arabs' strong and immovable rock.[21]

Therefore, although the Government of Kuwait had prepared a detailed draft of the agreement – including the type of pipes, capacity, means of protection and the pumping location – it had decided to withdraw from the project.[22] It also refused to link the pipeline question with the border adjustment issue, or the alternative of leasing this border area to Iraq. Nor would they accept the demarcation of the borders between the two countries as a precondition to agreement over any other issues.[23]

The open threat: Iraq's determination to absorb Kuwait

In 1958, political polarization between the Arab nationalist camp, led by Egypt's Nasser, had resulted in the creation of the United Arab Republic (UAR). In response, the Hashemite kingdoms, Iraq and Jordan, led by Iraq's Nouri As-Sa'eed, created a counter Arab Union on 14 February 1958. Iraq tried, without success, to persuade Kuwait to join the Hashemite Union and exerted great political and diplomatic pressure to accomplish this goal.

The Iraqi Government used every means, from inducements to threats, with the aim of securing a number of objectives. The first was expanding the Union's membership from two to three, giving the impression that it was the rising force in the Arab political community. The second was to extend the Union to include states that were not ruled by a Hashemite monarch. Without Kuwait's participation, it would appear to be nothing more than an internal family arrangement. Third, and most significant, it would unlock Kuwait's financial resources in support of the Union. Despite all the inducements and threats, Sheikh Abdullah Mubarak announced on his visit to Iraq in May 1958 that, 'Kuwait does not intend to join the Arab [Hashemite] Union'.[24]

In its attempts to urge Kuwait to join the Union, Iraq proposed a Brotherhood and Alliance Agreement between the Union governments and Kuwait, on the basis of guaranteeing the emirate's independence and its existing regime. This agreement would entail several major changes, including consultation in all matters relating to foreign affairs; Kuwait's representation abroad would be by the Union government's diplomatic and consular representatives. Kuwait would assist in confronting any aggression directed against a Union member, and contribute a fixed percentage to the Union's budget.

In 1958, Iraq Foreign Minister Tawfiq Al-Suweidi delivered a memorandum to both the United States and Britain, formally recognizing Kuwait's independence, provided it joined the Arab Union. In the event of Kuwait rejecting the proposal, Iraq requested reconsideration of Kuwait's borders with a view to returning Kuwait to its former status when 'it did not go far beyond Kuwait city'. If neither of these two proposals was accepted, then Iraq reserved its right to undertake any action it deemed appropriate.[25]

Nouri As-Sa'eed also contacted the United States Government, asking it to take positive steps, through the British Government, to convince Kuwait of the value of joining the Hashemite Arab Union. This would be on the basis that the Union needed strengthening, and Kuwait would provide the necessary strength.[26] London certainly exerted its influence to convince Kuwait to join the Union. In February 1958, Sir George Middleton, the British Ambassador in Lebanon, and Sir Bernard Burrows, the Political Resident in the Gulf, visited Kuwait to discuss the matter with the Emir. According to an American report, when Sir George Middleton met him, the Emir showed him a Lebanese newspaper that said that Kuwait had been joined with Iraq, and asked if that was the reason behind his visit to Kuwait. The Emir also listened to the British Resident's opinion; Burrows was cautious, spoke in general terms and did not commit himself to a fixed view.[27]

In March 1958, the Emir of Kuwait visited Iraq. Nouri As-Sa'eed offered to settle the border issue between the two countries and to provide Kuwait with water from Shatt Al-Arab, in return for joining the Union.[28] The Emir declined the offer and informed Nouri As-Sa'eed of his plan to visit Egypt after Nasser's return from Moscow. During the same month, and while the British Foreign Secretary was visiting Baghdad, Iraqi Prime Minster Fadel Al-Jamali stressed the need to declare Kuwait's independence and grant its Emir the title of 'King', to bring him to the same status as the two Hashemite monarchs, in return for joining the Union. On another occasion, the Union's Minister of Finance hinted to the US Ambassador that Iraq was ready to reach an agreement over the border problem and to guarantee the Emir's financial status in return for joining the Union. Negotiations took place between the kings of both Iraq and Jordan, and Abdullah Mubarak for Kuwait, but Kuwait would not change its position.

In June 1958, Nouri As-Sa'eed visited London to convince the Foreign Secretary, Selwyn Lloyd, that Kuwait should join the Union. The British Ambassador in Baghdad informed the Union's Foreign Minister that his government approved, in principle, the idea of Kuwait joining the Union. This was provided, however, that it should only take place after Kuwait's declaration of independence, and that an agreement on details would be reached in a meeting to be held in London on 24 July 1958.

In early July, it was obvious that London had taken a decision on Kuwait joining the Arab Union. This decision became clear when the British Foreign Secretary declared that Iraq should deal with Kuwait directly. This statement placed political pressure on Kuwait, especially when the Emir and his deputy became aware of the contents of a British memorandum on the subject. The statement meant that although Britain was not directly involved in the matter, it was in effect giving the green light to Iraq to exercise pressure on Kuwait.[29] In his meeting with the Emir, the Acting Political Agent talked about Kuwait's direct interest in a strong regime in Iraq. The Arab Union was an effective challenge to Nasser's expansionist policy, and Kuwait's joining would buttress it. When the Ruler asked what would happen to Kuwait if the Union failed, he received no clear answer to his question.[30]

In the light of all this pressure to come into line with the policy interests of the United States and the United Kingdom, Sheikh Abdullah Mubarak, as Deputy Ruler, made a dramatic intervention. He publicly stated that Kuwait 'can and perhaps may join the United Arab Republic. That is not impossible to achieve while still maintaining a special relationship with Britain.'[31]

The British Government moved quickly to counteract his unexpected démarche. The Foreign Office prepared a detailed memorandum listing the advantages of Kuwait joining the Arab Union. It contained the following: 'Kuwait maintains its independent legal personality, its regime, its flag in its territory, and the Union's flag as its official flag abroad. Citizens of member states of the Union shall have the rights of ownership, movement, residence, work and study in the educational institutions of the three states.'

This document reflected the objectives of the Iraqi and Jordanian governments and their insistence on Kuwait joining the Union, which would mean that Iraq and Jordan would benefit from Kuwait's financial resources. The memo assumed Kuwait's agreement to the proposal that the Union's government should have responsibility for exercising a number of powers. These included foreign affairs, the armed forces, customs, currency and foreign exchange in all the states of the Arab Union. In an attempt to give Kuwait the impression that it would not be compromising its sovereignty, the memo indicated that consultation with the Emir of Kuwait on all matters related to Kuwait's foreign affairs and defence would take place before any final decision was made.[32]

However, fate intervened. The 14 July 1958 revolution in Baghdad, led by an Iraqi general, Abdul Karim Qassem, put an end to Hashemite rule in Iraq and to the Arab Union, and opened a new chapter in relations between Kuwait and Iraq.

The 1958 revolution: renewed pressure on Kuwait

When the Iraqi revolution broke out, Sheikh Abdullah Mubarak was on holiday abroad, and upon hearing the news he returned home immediately. Initially the British and Americans reserved their position pending clarification on how the revolution might affect Kuwait, both internally and externally. Their concerns seemed in the weeks following the revolution to be unfounded. For instance, the American Consul in Kuwait sent a telegram on 23 July informing the Department of State that the popular jubilation for the revolution had quickly faded and no demonstrations or disturbance had taken place.

Nevertheless, Abdullah Mubarak thought that such a fundamental change in Iraq, with all the political tension with Kuwait, warranted immediate security measures. He declared a state of emergency in the army, and checked on the army's preparedness on a daily basis. He instructed his main assistants in public security and in the army, Sheikh Mubarak al-Ahmed Al-Sabah and Sheikh Mubarak al-Jaber Al-Sabah respectively, to create a night-duty roster at Public Security Headquarters in order to be able to act quickly in the event of any emergency. This high state of alert lasted for several weeks after the revolution.[33]

Kuwait extended a hand of friendship to the new regime and Sheikh Abdullah Mubarak declared that the Iraqi revolution came as 'a victory for the will of the Iraqi people and for its right to live with its Arab brothers ... we supported the Iraqi Revolution from the first moment after the United Arab Republic had recognized it. Perhaps, no one knows that my aircraft was the only aircraft that the Revolution allowed to fly in the Iraqi sky on the first day of the Revolution.'[34] In a meeting with the American Consul and the Political Agent, Sheikh Abdullah Mubarak mentioned that Nouri As-Sa'eed's mistake was to deprive the Iraqi people of the benefits of oil, which were channelled instead to the elite. He compared this with the Kuwaiti Government's policy which rewarded both rich and poor.[35]

Abdullah Mubarak visited Baghdad at the invitation of General Abdul Karim Qassem and held talks about bilateral relations; as a result of their meeting, the Iraqi Government lifted the sanctions on exporting food to Kuwait.[36]

The Emir visited Iraq in October and discussed the demarcation of borders, the exchange of security information and criminals, and Kuwaiti investment in Iraq.[37] However, the honeymoon soon came to an end. With Abdul Karim Qassem adopting the communist line, the talk about a greater Iraq, and the export of revolutionary and leftist ideas, relations with Kuwait became strained.

Sheikh Abdullah Mubarak, as head of public security, put in place special measures to protect the border from infiltration by communists from outside, and watched their activities inside Kuwait. He deported a number of Iraqi communists, who were accused of fomenting riots.[38] Abdullah Mubarak did not fear any Iraqi reactions to his measures; nor did he respond to the intervention of some Kuwaiti merchants who advised him to discontinue the policy so as to avoid Iraqi reprisals.[39] When Kuwait's security was threatened, Abdullah Mubarak always acted decisively and with confidence. US documents indicate that in March 1959, when he received reports about the activity of Iraqi communists in Kuwait, he said: 'Our prisons still have room for communists and trouble-makers.'[40]

At a lunch party in the US Consulate in May 1959, Abdullah Mubarak said he had received a message from the Iraqi authorities, through a member of the Al-Sabah family who was in Basra, asking why he (Sheikh Abdullah Mubarak) did not visit Baghdad and why he did not approve the Shatt Al-Arab water project. He answered by saying that Iraq had fallen into communist hands and was already beyond salvation: 'In my heart I felt like telling them that I would neither visit Iraq nor agree to any such water schemes as long as the present situation prevails in Iraq.'[41] When Abdullah Mubarak was asked to attend the first anniversary of the July revolution, he would not accept an invitation from a regime undertaking bloody liquidations of its political opponents.[42]

Although he received several requests to visit Baghdad, he turned them all down, as long as the anti-Kuwait stand continued.[43] He was wise enough, however, not to break all ties with the Qassem regime.[44] He distinguished clearly between the Iraqi Government and the Iraqi people, his view being that the tense political relations between the two governments should not affect the brotherly ties between their people. Therefore he declared in December 1959 to the *Iraq Times* that the Kuwaiti people appreciated the Iraqi people's efforts for progress and prosperity and that relations between the two states should be strengthened in this fraternal atmosphere.

He stressed the deep brotherly relations between Iraq and Kuwait by declaring: 'Those relations were not ordinary relations similar to those existing between any two states, but warm, brotherly connections based on strong and long-standing links supported by mutual understanding and good neighbourly ties.' He referred to the large Iraqi community in Kuwait, saying:

> We like Iraq and the Iraqis and we always seek to provide comfort to our Iraqi brothers working in Kuwait, welcoming them and providing them with job opportunities. We have never discriminated between them and the Kuwaitis and we treat them as brothers, we consider them as part of our people. Our relations will expand more; we encourage these relations in all fields. There are many Iraqi students in our schools. The highway between Kuwait and Iraq is paved in such a way that would enhance communications between the two states and encourage bilateral traffic ... we would like to encourage our commercial ties with Iraq.

He added: 'We hope that the difficult agricultural conditions of last year are at an end, so that we can import our needs from Iraq. We also want Iraq to accept some of our needs. We seek good relations with our neighbours. We are sincere friends to the other Arab states neighbouring Kuwait, and we will not permit conversion of Kuwait into a base from which attacks against any Arab state can be launched.'[45]

In March 1960, Abdul Karim Qassem invited Abdullah Mubarak to visit Baghdad to discuss the issues between the two countries and to consider Iraq's desire to open a consulate in Kuwait.[46] However, there is no evidence, in the press or in diplomatic documents, that the visit occurred. The two men finally met again in 1961, when Abdullah Mubarak travelled on 26 March to attend the celebration of the opening of the new port at Umm Qasr. On this occasion, Qassem's behaviour towards Kuwait was cordial and he commended Abdullah Mubarak's keenness to attend: 'The Iraqi people belong to Kuwait and the new port will be for mutual cooperation and benefit.' The Iraqi officials promised to expedite the construction of an express motorway between Umm Qasr and Safwan, and that this motorway should take priority over the Umm Qasr and Basra route.[47] However, with the declaration of Kuwait's independence on 19 June 1961, the old Iraqi ambitions returned with a military move on the border with Kuwait, and events yet again took a new and dangerous turn.

Denying Kuwait's right to independence

Six days after the declaration of Kuwait's independence, Qassem held a press conference at the Iraqi Ministry of Defence, explicitly demanding the annexation of Kuwait. It was, he declared, a district forming part of the Basra district and, as such, an integral part of Iraq. He asked Abdullah Mubarak to cooperate with him to restore things to their normal course. He also announced that Iraq would not relinquish one single inch of Kuwait's territory — and he had the power to enforce what he said.

On 26 June, the Iraqi Foreign Ministry summoned representatives of the diplomatic missions in Baghdad and handed them an official memorandum reiterating claims that Kuwait was part of the Basra district. It claimed that the 19 June 1961 agreement represented an extension of British protection over Kuwait. In response to that, the Secretariat of the Government of Kuwait issued a statement saying: 'Kuwait is an independent Arab state, with full sovereignty and international recognition. The Government of Kuwait, backed by the whole Kuwaiti people, is determined to defend and protect Kuwait's independence.'

Kuwait declared a state of emergency and deployed more forces on the border. It consulted with Britain, and an agreement was reached to postpone the evacuation of the British forces and the British naval units from Kuwait. Meanwhile, Iraqi forces seized 10 Kuwaiti ships docked at Basra. The Iraqi Government also froze the funds of Kuwaiti citizens at Iraqi banks, as well as severing diplomatic relations with states that recognized the Kuwaiti Government, such as Lebanon, the United States, Iran, Jordan, Japan and Tunisia.

Another dimension of the crisis emerged during the discussion of Kuwait's application to join the Arab League. When the League's council met in an emergency session on 5 July 1961, it failed to adopt a resolution because of divisions among the member states. While Saudi Arabia strongly supported Kuwait's application, and threatened to withdraw in the event that the council rejected the application, Iraq on the other hand opposed the request and threatened withdrawal in the event it was accepted. After intensive negotiations, the Arab League issued a statement on 20 July welcoming Kuwait's membership and pledging assistance for Kuwait to join the United Nations.

At the same time, the statement contained a provision committing Kuwait to request the withdrawal of British forces from Kuwait, as soon as possible, and the commitment of the Iraqi Government not to resort to force against Kuwait. The Arab League sent forces to preserve peace on the Iraqi–Kuwaiti borders after the withdrawal of the British forces. On 10 October 1961, Kuwait announced the complete withdrawal of the British forces.

Although this crisis occurred after Abdullah Mubarak had resigned and settled in Lebanon, he returned to Kuwait immediately after hearing the news and put himself at the disposal of his country. Sensing that his presence could cause embarrassment, he returned to Lebanon and used all his formal and informal connections in support of Kuwait's independence. He called President Nasser to ask for his direct intervention. He also sent messages to all Arab leaders with whom he had close relations, requesting their support for Kuwait and warning of the serious consequences of any Iraqi aggression. Their support was also sought for Kuwait's request to join the Arab League. On the popular front, he mobilized close links with the Lebanese press to impact on Arab public opinion against Iraqi threats, which would have an adverse impact on Arab solidarity and the future of inter-Arab relations.

Although Sheikh Abdullah Mubarak was no longer in power at this point, Kuwait's military strategy and coordination plans with Britain had been drawn up under his direct supervision. Despite the false claims circulated then and after his resignation, Abdullah Mubarak had planned for every eventuality and discussed with the British military authorities the various likely scenarios for Iraqi threats. Intervention plans in case of foreign aggression against Kuwait were fully prepared. Abdullah Mubarak had begun consultations with London far in advance regarding cooperation and coordination, in preparing defensive plans for Kuwait and agreeing the level of military assistance it would obtain.

These efforts resulted in the British Government's offer of military assistance to the State of Kuwait. Sir Herbert Batch, the commander of the British forces in Arabia, had earlier written a letter on 12 May 1960 to Abdullah Mubarak, stating: 'I have the honour to send your Highness the plans relevant to providing the British military assistance to your country when requested by H.H. the Ruler of Kuwait.'

The letter went on to discuss the practical steps to that effect, both politically and militarily:

> We hope to receive your warning at least four days before the outbreak of operations, to give our forces adequate time for grouping; however, our detailed plans enable us to assist you even if we do not receive your warning. Therefore, your Highness must certainly appreciate the great significance we attach to receiving the request of H.H. the Ruler at an early time requesting our assistance because carrying out a plan before completing our mobilization might create a risky military situation.

As for the military details, they contained all the defensive dimensions: land, air and sea, all of which were in the form of assistance conditional on the approval of the Ruler of Kuwait. The British commander's letter provided the following:

> Targets in Kuwait might be vulnerable to air raids in the early stages of any aggression. We are currently conducting a detailed study for installing a radar set to provide air defence for Kuwait's air space. I hope that your Highness will approve installing a radar set in Kuwait when we submit our recommendation. The success of our plans also depends on using Kuwait's airport and port for the entry of our forces. It also depends on the Kuwaiti authorities providing the British forces with most of their transportation, and all vehicle and aircraft fuel. Our forces will need the facilities in hospitals and will need workers, warehouses, workshops and systems for producing fresh water. These requirements have been discussed with H.E. Sheikh Mubarak Al-Abdullah Al-Jaber Al-Sabah [sic]
>
> Air raids may render the ports unfit for operation for a short time. Then, it would become necessary to unload the equipment on the shores, which are unprepared for

unloading goods in Kuwait. Therefore, to ensure a successful operation, the shoreline must be surveyed as quickly as possible.

Until that happens, no guarantee can be given to the unloading of heavy equipment and the ammunition required for our plans in Kuwait. If the operation extends further beyond a few days, the lack of these facilities ... [might give cause that] the operation might fail entirely.

In the end, the letter reaffirms:

Finally, I would like to confirm to your Highness that our mutual cooperation is necessary for the implementation of these plans which we shall review periodically in the light of developments.

The resemblance between events of 1960–1 and the period preceding the Iraqi invasion of Kuwait in 1990 is striking. On the other hand, the contrast between the measures adopted then and those adopted after the invasion in 1990 is also striking. It seems that history sometimes repeats itself, but lessons are not always learned.

After the arrest, trial and immediate execution of Abdul Karim Qassem and the end of his regime on 8 February 1963, relations between Iraq and Kuwait began to improve. Discussions between the prime ministers of the two states took place in Baghdad and were concluded by the signing of a joint agreement on 4 October 1963. The main terms were:

- Iraq's recognition of the independence of Kuwait and its complete sovereignty over its border, as confirmed in the letter of the Iraqi Prime Minister dated 21 July 1932.

- Establishing prompt diplomatic relations at ambassa-
  dorial level.
- Enhancing bilateral brotherly relations at all levels, in
  accordance with their long mutual historic ties and
  links.
- Supplying Kuwait with 120 million gallons of water
  per day from the Shatt Al-Arab.
- In return, Kuwait granted Iraq an interest-free loan of
  KD 30 million. But Kuwait was still not enthusiastic
  about obtaining water from Iraq, in order to avoid the
  risk of too heavy a dependence on a neighbouring state
  for such a strategic resource.

Although the 1963 agreement resulted in Iraq's recognition of
Kuwait's independence and sovereignty, it did not put an end to
the border problems between the two countries. New
discussions between the two states were held in 1964 and
1965 in order to demarcate borders, but without tangible
results. In 1965, President Abdul-Salam Aref made another
request to lease Warba island for 99 years. Kuwait rejected the
request. In 1966, a crisis broke out between the two countries
when an Iraqi military division entered Bubiyan island in
protest against the negotiations between Iran and Kuwait
without Iraqi participation. In 1967, a fresh crisis occurred
when an Iraqi force crossed the border and attacked some
Kuwaiti Bedouins between Al-Abdali and Safwan. The crisis
was contained, after Iraq obtained a loan of KD 25 million
from Kuwait.

After the Ba'ath Party came to power in Iraq in 1968 it aimed
to normalize relations with Kuwait without demarcating
borders. But with Iran's unilateral termination of the 1937
border agreement with Iraq and the escalated tension on Shatt

Al-Arab in 1969, Iraq requested that Kuwait should allow some Iraqi forces to be deployed on Kuwaiti territories to defend Umm Qasr port against probable Iranian attacks. In fact, an unwritten agreement was reached, with some Iraqi forces entering Kuwaiti territories.

During these years, Abdullah Mubarak's efforts continued to support Kuwait's interests. He maintained his relations with a number of Iraqi desert tribes. During his visit to Iraq in 1965, he received the tribal sheikhs in Al-Ramadi, Al-Najaf and Al-Hella, who competed with each other in offering gifts (as a sign of respect). Among the precious gifts he received from the Al-Ramadi sheikhs were a number of noble Arab horses that he sent to Egypt (where he was living).

Abdullah Mubarak used his extensive network of contacts to keep informed about all the latest developments. With every crisis he made contact with friends in high places, monarchs and political leaders, asking them to intervene and exert pressure on Iraq. Constant communication passed between him and the Emir of Kuwait, relaying information pertaining to Kuwait's security.

From the 1973 crisis to military invasion in 1990

Relations between the two countries again became tense in 1972, when Kuwait refused an Iraqi request for a sizeable loan. In March 1973, another crisis occurred when Iraqi forces attacked two border control offices in the north-east of Kuwait and penetrated 3 kilometres into Kuwaiti territory. The attack resulted in the death or injury of a number of Kuwaiti policemen. Consequently, Kuwait declared a state of emergency and closed its border with Iraq; the Kuwait National Assembly asked Iraq to withdraw its forces from Kuwaiti territory immediately.

At the instigation of the Arab League, and a number of states that used their good offices, discussions between the foreign ministers of the two states began in Kuwait on 6 April 1973 in order to settle the fresh border crisis. However, the two sides did not agree on anything regarding the demarcation of borders, although Iraq withdrew from the post (Al-Samta) after it had obtained a sizeable loan.

After the signing of the Algiers Agreement between Iran and Iraq in 1975, according to which Iraq relinquished part of Shatt Al-Arab to Iran, Iraq again asked Kuwait to lease half of Bubiyan island for 99 years and to relinquish Warba island in return for its recognition of the existing border between the two countries. But Kuwait rejected the Iraqi demand. Further futile talks took place between the two sides in order to reach an agreement on the demarcation of the frontier.

The outbreak of the Islamic Revolution in Iran in 1979 and the Iran–Iraq War in 1980 froze the border problem between the two countries. This, however, did not prevent Iraq from requesting the lease of Warba and Bubiyan islands in 1981 and 1990. It requested military facilities in Kuwait in 1984 and 1986, with a view to strengthening its military position against Iran. Kuwait was unenthusiastic about these requests, although it adopted a posture of unequivocal support for Iraq both at the governmental level and with regard to public opinion. This position infuriated Iran, especially when Kuwait offered economic aid and loans to Iraq on a huge scale during the Iran–Iraq conflict.

After the end of the Iran–Iraq War, Kuwait looked forward to reaching a final settlement of the border with Iraq, especially in light of Iraqi officials' promises regarding that problem during the war. But Iraq used delaying tactics and acted in a way that reflected its desire to continue blackmailing Kuwait without reaching a solution.

Iraq asked Kuwait to write off its debts and to offer a loan of US$10 billion. Kuwait refused the first demand, but declared its readiness to offer a loan of US$500 million, provided that a committee for the demarcation of borders was set up.

Iraq continued creating tension between the two countries, accusing Kuwait of pumping and marketing the crude oil from the Iraqi Rumeilah oilfield. It also accused Kuwait of moving the border signs to the north, thus cutting off parts of Iraqi territory. It was these specious allegations that provided the basis for the Iraqi invasion of Kuwait in August 1990.

–6–

The Resignation of Abdullah Mubarak

When Sheikh Abdullah Mubarak left political life in April 1961, there were many rumours in Kuwait and the Arab world about the reasons for his resignation. Determined to preserve the unity and cohesion of the Al-Sabah family, he did not refute the charges and speculation published by Arab newspapers even when Kuwaiti sources had leaked them. He opted for a complete and dignified silence, simply adhering to the principles that had run through his entire political life. In fact, the Sheikh's resignation cannot be understood unless it is viewed in its historical context and in the light of his political and moral principles.

Abdullah Mubarak voluntarily abandoned the attractions of power and authority. He did not lobby with or against anyone, nor did he try to exert pressure on anyone or employ the tools of power and influence under his control. Rather, at the peak of his authority he withdrew quietly, proud of his political achievements.

So what could have caused him to leave his post? The historical fact, clearly illustrated in this book, is that by the late 1950s he had become Deputy Ruler and the most prominent political personality in Kuwait. He occupied this dominant position because of his competence, long service and extra-ordinary experience of most aspects of Kuwaiti life. No doubt, when Kuwait's history in the twentieth century is written, Abdullah Mubarak will occupy a pre-eminent position. However, he will feature not only in the history of Kuwait, as he also firmly believed in the great cause of the Arabs and espoused the cause of Arabism with an absolute commitment. The Kuwaitis nicknamed him the 'Falcon of the Gulf' and his legacy continues to this day.

It might seem that the villains of this book were the British officials in Kuwait – and to some degree perhaps they were. Britain took on the role of 'protecting' Kuwait at the beginning of the twentieth century in order to protect its own position at the head of the Gulf. It was a sensible but self-interested political act; the British Government extended 'protection' to many other communities in the region because it gave them control of a sea route to their Indian empire at a very low cost.

Under the provisions of the 1899 agreement Britain handled Kuwait's foreign relations, ensuring that Kuwait's communica-tions with other countries passed through British officials. Therefore, London viewed the Sheikh's Arab and international contacts with concern. The British role did not stop at foreign affairs and, with Kuwait's vastly increased wealth, London was no longer satisfied with its traditional position under the protection agreement as practised by the Political Agents in Kuwait over many years, a practice that was generally characterized by non-intervention in domestic affairs.

With the expansion in oil production in 1953, the British Gulf Resident received specific instructions from London to monitor the domestic situation in Kuwait, to protect British interests, and to oversee economic development and construction activities in order to help British companies get a major share in contracts. He was also to follow up the creation of new government departments, or expansion in the existing departments, to ensure that they were developed in accordance with British advice and under a British advisor's supervision.

In August 1955, the first assessment of the situation in Kuwait undertaken by Pelly, the new British Political Agent, defined British interests as: securing continuity in oil production; continued payment in sterling, and spending the major portion of oil revenues to buy goods, services or shares and bonds in sterling; and helping British companies to obtain major contracts in Kuwait.[1]

To that end, London granted the Political Agent in Kuwait wide discretionary powers, a larger staff and allowed him to communicate with London directly rather than through the Political Resident in Bahrain.

Leaving power behind

Abdullah Mubarak was only 46 years old, and at the zenith of his career, when he retired from Kuwaiti political life just three months before independence in 1961. He had always desired a Kuwait free of foreign domination. A free Kuwait was the fulfilment of all his efforts in the 1940s and 1950s, which had provided the preconditions for independence. It was unimaginable for Kuwait to be independent without having the facilities of a modern state. Independence was not a slogan or a legal status, but a political reality centred on the ability to govern, which could only be achieved through modern institutions. The basis for Kuwait's independence was the period of Sheikh Abdullah Mubarak's building of the nation's institutions – a modern army, security and police departments, aviation, radio, modern communications – thus providing the foundation of a modern state.

Matters that we take for granted today were not so before his work. For instance, when Lebanon wanted to open an honorary consulate in Kuwait in 1953 it had to submit its application to the British Embassy in Beirut.[2] The Political Agent objected to the application because British policy was against any foreign representation in the Gulf Emirates, which should fall under the protection agreement. The presence of foreign consulates represented 'a serious threat to our position in Kuwait'.[3] The trend of increasing British interference in Kuwait's domestic affairs led to more confrontation and friction between the Sheikh and the Political Agent.

Sheikh Abdullah Mubarak's resignation was closely connected with the activity of the British Government. The communications between London and the Political Agency in Kuwait provide an intermittent account of a power conflict within the ruling family and an appraisal of each party to this conflict, along with their chances. The same kind of *idée fixe* of plotting and *coup d'état* occur in the British records for other states such as Bahrain and Abu Dhabi.[4] Within that context, I shall first review the reports of the British Political Agent in Kuwait in this situation, and then convey what I learned from Abdullah Mubarak on the subject.

The British records of the Al-Sabah succession

A reader of the British diplomatic reports on Kuwait might be surprised by the preponderance of succession issues and the way in which they present rivalry among the sheikhs. They leave the reader with the impression that the main, if not the only concern of those sheikhs was personal rivalry. How the British diplomats evaluated the different political players – the basis for each evaluation and the occasional change in the evaluation – is difficult to ascertain. The surprising matter remains the concentration and insistence on what those reports termed 'the rivalry for power'. In the Gulf, these issues came into sharpest focus whenever the realistic likelihood of a change of ruler – through age or infirmity – seemed greatest. In Kuwait, however, speculation was often alarmist without any sound cause.

Perhaps we should ask why these documents were written. The Political Agents in the Gulf wrote for their masters in London, and told them the story they wanted to hear. Throughout the Gulf, the story was more or less the same: a good Arab was one who did what the British officials wanted, who made their working lives easier by willingly conforming to all the twists and turns of British policy in the region. Those who resisted or would not agree were presented as trouble-makers – wicked, obstructive, malign, self-serving and corrupt.

The traditions of the British officials in the Gulf developed from the governmental culture of British India rather than that of the Foreign Office in London. One of those traditions was caution and prudence, not taking any chances. A Political Agent who warned of dire consequences and painted the blackest picture, drawing the most negative conclusions, would never be deemed wrong. Any Political Agent who failed to warn

London, or became too close to the Arabs, was likely to be regarded as naive or inadequate by the standards of the service. It was the Political Resident's task to ensure that the appropriate message was sent home to London. If we are to read the reports from Kuwait with an acceptance of those terms, it is perhaps easier to understand why Abdullah Mubarak was cast in such a demonic light.

There is a comparable situation in another Gulf state under British control. The year after Abdullah Mubarak resigned, the Emir of Bahrain, Sheikh Salman bin Hamad Al-Khalifa, died. Like Sheikh Abdullah Mubarak he had been a perpetual thorn in the side of the British authorities. He too was subjected to constant innuendo and outright denunciation in the British reports and in the diary of his advisor. In the eyes of the British, both men's failure was their complete inability to follow loyally the twists and turns of British policy, however inept or misguided. Unfortunately, they had minds of their own, which was a cardinal sin in the eye of the British Government and its officials.

In this situation, we may imagine the impact of Abdullah Mubarak's statements such as 'the Arab countries are for the Arabs'; his support for the Syrian and Egyptian armies; his cancellation of the entry visas (to Kuwait) for the Arabs; his support of the nationalization of the Suez Canal Company; and his zeal for Arab solidarity and unity.

However, the situation in Kuwait was more serious than in Bahrain, and of longer duration. In the early 1940s, the Political Agent's reports from Kuwait indicated the emergence of rivalry between three parties: the sons of Ahmed al-Jaber, Sheikh Abdullah Al-Salem and his supporters, and 'one person', Abdullah Mubarak, the son of Sheikh Mubarak Al-Sabah. The reports explained this unbalanced family rivalry between two major groups of the Al-Sabahs and 'one person' by the fact that the latter was the son of the founder of modern Kuwait, and the uncle of the ruling Emir, that is Sheikh Ahmed al-Jaber, despite his youth and that he was effectively the 'uncle' of all the Al-Sabah sheikhs.[5]

In a report by Political Agent Galloway concerning the political situation in Kuwait, dated 19 January 1949, he began by saying: 'One thing is certain, namely, a conflict for succession will happen and might lead to the actual use of weapons.'[6] There was a general agreement on Sheikh Ahmed al-Jaber, and that if Sheikh Abdullah Mubarak tried to use force, he would be opposed by the merchants and the police force controlled by Sheikh Sabah Al-Salem, the brother of the anticipated Emir.

Thus, at this point the British reports raised doubts and fears about Abdullah Mubarak's position and the possibility of him resorting to a *coup d'état* to take the position of ruler. They continued to offer their dire premonitions at intervals until his resignation in 1961.

The first occasion when the British reports focused on the succession issue was in 1950, with the worsening state of Sheikh Ahmed al-Jaber's health. On 18 January 1950, the Political Agent reported the deterioration of his condition and that Sheikh Abdullah Al-Salem was on his way to India and Sheikh Abdullah Mubarak was receiving guests at the Ruler's palace. If the Emir passed away, he added, Sheikh Abdullah Mubarak 'would seek his succession'. That might lead to a clash between the police force and public security, and in that case it would be likely that the British forces would intervene to restore order. The Political Agent did not leave any doubt about Sheikh Abdullah Mubarak's intentions and asserted that, if the Ruler died while Sheikh Abdullah Al-Salem was abroad, 'there is no doubt that Mubarak will seize the opportunity to become the next ruler'.[7]

The Political Agent's evaluation was that Sheikh Abdullah Mubarak enjoyed the support of the Badiya (desert tribes) and controlled a large military force.[8] The evaluation of the US Consul in Basra was that Sheikh Abdullah Al-Salem was the leading candidate for ruler and that Sheikh Abdullah Mubarak was his strongest competitor because he enjoyed Badiya support. It was further stated that the oil companies 'fear him and do not want him to be the ruler', and that the British Political Agent and the Westerners, in general, cannot trust him. He added that: 'The prevailing belief in Kuwait among the British and the Westerners is that Mubarak hates the British, and the Political Agent and the Agency staff expressed their displeasure with, and lack of admiration for Abdullah Mubarak.'[9]

Although a member of the ruling family discussed the issue with the Political Agent and confirmed to him the existence of well-established traditions and norms regarding succession within the Al-Sabah family, and that Sheikh Abdullah Mubarak would not challenge Sheikh Abdullah Al-Salem, the British authorities expected, on the basis of their doubts and fears, a disturbance in Kuwait. Therefore, a British warship was instructed to remain offshore, and the commander of the British land forces in the Middle East declared a state of emergency, to be ready for rapid intervention if the situation warranted it.[10]

Indeed, 30 armoured vehicles moved from the Al-Habaniya base in Iraq and took up positions near Basra, ready to move into Kuwait if necessary. The Political Agent also ordered the oil company to adopt precautionary measures to confront 'any emerging situations'. The company evicted the families of some of its employees and transferred its documents to other places. According to the US Consul's report, those measures were to counter any attempt by Sheikh Abdullah Mubarak to seize power. In one of the consul's reports, he mentioned that the British Resident in Bahrain had informed him that the British adopted the necessary measures out of fear of what Deputy Ruler Sheikh Abdullah Mubarak would do after the Ruler's death.[11]

If we move from the Anglo-American fears, concerns and precautionary measures to what actually took place on the Emir's death, an entirely different story emerges. Sheikh Ahmed al-Jaber died at the Dasman Palace at 7.15 p.m. on 29 January 1950. He was 64. Sheikh Abdullah Mubarak, as Deputy Ruler, immediately took control of the situation. He instructed the radio officials to broadcast the news, asked citizens to close their shops, and national mourning was declared. Public security forces patrolled the city streets. Simultaneously, he sent a message to Sheikh Abdullah Al-Salem requesting his immediate return.

At 8.00 a.m. the next morning, the funeral of the deceased Ruler took place, with Sheikh Abdullah Mubarak, senior members of the Al-Sabah, city notables and prominent merchants taking part. According to the US Consul's estimate, about 75,000 people took part in the funeral procession.

On the morning of 31 January the new ruler, Sheikh Abdullah Al-Salem, returned by ship and was received by Sheikh Abdullah Mubarak who then took him to the Public Security Headquarters, where they received citizens' condolences. The US Consul reported that Sheikh Abdullah Mubarak performed all procedures without consulting Britain, thus ignoring the special relationship linking Kuwait with Britain.[12]

On 25 February Sheikh Abdullah Al-Salem became the new Emir; Sheikh Abdullah Mubarak supervised all the coronation arrangements, with a major celebration at Safat Square. According to the Political Agent, Sheikh Abdullah Mubarak told the Ruler, 'Everything was done as you wish', which was interpreted to mean his expression of loyalty and his readiness to work loyally under the Ruler's leadership.[13]

Most probably, the British Political Agent reached the same conclusion as the US Consul, namely that Sheikh Abdullah Mubarak's disregard for rules of the special British–Kuwaiti relationship confirmed all his doubts about Abdullah Mubarak's attitude to the British connection. Britain was very strict in its recognition of a new ruler in Kuwait and his compliance with the treaty undertaking in respect of contacts with other states. In the period between the coronation of Sheikh Abdullah Al-Salem and the British Government's recognition, the Political Agent exercised his influence to prohibit any foreign official from visiting the Ruler. For example, when Commodore Hensell, commander of an American frigate docking at Kuwait Port, wanted to visit the Ruler to salute him, the Political Agent agreed only after some hesitation. During the visit, Hensell invited the Ruler to dinner aboard the ship but the Political Agent objected because the ship would then fire a 21-gun salute upon the Ruler's arrival, which could not be allowed to happen until Britain had officially recognized him. The commodore solved the problem by sailing from the port before the scheduled date and sending an apology to the Ruler. A report by the US Consul in Basra about the matter said that he was not sure of the correctness of the British position and would visit Kuwait to verify its legal basis.[14]

It is surprising to find some English and Arabic sources containing inaccurate information about the events of that year. An example is Jamal Z. Qassem's book *The Arab Gulf: A Study of its Contemporary History 1945–1971*, which mentions that Sheikh Abdullah [Mubarak] 'planned a coup d'état attempt in 1950 but the attempt failed and the conspirator fled to Egypt'.[15]

It seems that the author's source for such allegations was a work by Salah Al-Aqqad entitled *Landmarks of Change in the Arabian Gulf States*. Both works relied upon an English language source called *Middle East Politics: The Military Dimension*, by J. C. Hurewitz, who was teaching at Columbia University in New York City. It is regrettable that what might appear to a reader as an authoritative piece of well-documented information is in fact a groundless and unsubstantiated account. In September 1951, the Political Agent analysed the Kuwait political map in light of what happened at the death of Sheikh Ahmed al-Jaber. He summarized the situation as follows:[16]

1. There were no specific rules or laws to select the ruler; the selection was based on agreement among members of the ruling family.

2. There were no prominent candidates or rivals for the succession of Sheikh Ahmed al-Jaber, apart from Sheikh Abdullah Al-Salem. He was the eldest, over 50, and obtained the approval of most members of the ruling family. Other candidates were under 40 years of age, except Sheikh Ahmed al-Jaber, the grandchild of Mubarak Al-Kabir's brother.

3. In the under-40 group, the most prominent candidate was Sheikh Abdullah Mubarak who had the advantage of being the direct son of Mubarak Al-Kabir, compared with Abdullah Al-Salem who was a grandchild. In other words, Sheikh Abdullah Mubarak was the Ruler's uncle; therefore, he comes directly next to him in the power and influence hierarchy and was the Emir's deputy.

4. The third person in the power hierarchy was Sheikh Abdullah Al-Ahmed, the grandchild of Sheikh Jaber Al-Mubarak and the elder son of Sheikh Ahmed al-Jaber. He worked as an assistant to Sheikh Abdullah Mubarak. Ruling was not among his immediate aspirations. He was quiet and pious and did not want to supplant his uncle (Abdullah Mubarak).

5. The two prominent characters within the same age group, and who rivalled Sheikh Abdullah Mubarak, according to the Political Agent's analysis, were Sheikh Fahad and Sheikh Sabah, who were half-brothers of Sheikh Abdullah Al-Salem.

On 12 October 1953, a number of Arab newspapers, quoting the Iraqi News Agency and *Lewa' Al-Istiqlal* newspaper in Baghdad, published headlines like: 'The Emir of Kuwait Forced to Resign';[17] 'A Military Gunboat Rushes To Kuwait'; 'Abdullah Mubarak undertook a Military Rebellion and Forced the Emir of Kuwait to Resign'. Immediately, the British Foreign Office announced that those stories were baseless;[18] Sheikh Abdullah Mubarak also denied his involvement in any rebellion.[19]

In a report by the British Ambassador in Baghdad, Abdullah Mubarak mentioned that when he met with Iraqi Prime Minister Fadel Al-Jamali, the latter began by questioning him about the news of the rebellion in Kuwait and the ambassador responded saying, 'the news came from Iraq'. Al-Jamali added that his government was criticized for its failure to take any action to protect Iraqi interests when the British moved quickly. He then wondered if Saudi Arabia was behind the *coup d'état* attempt, as a result of the close relationship between Abdullah Mubarak and King Saud.[20]

In the same year, it was rumoured in the Arabic press in Baghdad that Sheikh Abdullah Al-Salem had submitted his resignation in protest against the continued conflicts between Sheikh Abdullah Mubarak and Sheikh Fahad Al-Salem. Then he changed his mind.[21] We should pause here to note that the rumours about rifts and conflicts among Kuwait's sheikhs all came from Baghdad.

The truth, as illustrated by diplomatic reports, was that the news was unfounded. It is true that in the previous year (1952) Sheikh Abdullah Al-Salem talked to some friends about his desire to retire, due to his old age and increased responsibilities, and that he was considering resignation. The Political Resident wrote several reports during 1952 about the subject. To him, the Ruler threatened resignation so that others would accept his views, but he never intended to resign.[22] The US Embassy in London also wrote to Washington confirming that, based on its communications with the Foreign Office, all news agency reports about the Emir of Kuwait's resignation or the attempted *coup d'état* against him were rumours.[23]

The British fears continued amidst the speculation. In a report dated February 1955 about the probable candidates to rule Kuwait after Sheikh Abdullah Al-Salem, the Political Agent described the possibility of Sheikh Abdullah Mubarak becoming the ruler as a 'disaster' for Britain and that necessary measures should be taken to prevent him from seizing power by force.[24]

In his first report in the summer of 1955, the new Political Agent (Pelly) mentioned that in the event of the Ruler's death or abdication, Sheikh Abdullah Mubarak's position would be extremely strong. He added: 'I have no doubt that if he wants he will assume authority with or without a general support from the Al-Sabah family. By the same token, he can guarantee the role of Emir to the candidate he selects.' Pelly explained how Abdullah Mubarak's power was a result of his extensive influence within the family, stemming from the military power he controlled, and it could not be challenged.[25]

Two years later, the Political Agent wrote on 17 January 1957 that in the event of the Ruler's death, there was a high probability that in such a case Abdullah Mubarak might seize power by force and 'we should be ready to act quickly and decisively and at the earliest possible moment'.[26]

In his analysis of the situation and the prospects of succession, the Political Agent defined, in his report dated 19 November 1958, five scenarios:[27]

1. Quiet elections by which the Al-Sabahs select a competent man. This is the best option to secure Kuwait's stability.

2. A conflict breaking out between Sheikh Abdullah Mubarak and Sheikh Fahad Al-Salem with a resort to force. Abdullah Mubarak is stronger by virtue of his dominance over the armed forces and Fahad Al-Salem is his main rival and the strongest family member. Because the Kuwaiti public opinion was not decisive [between the candidates], that will open the door for Abdullah Mubarak to carry out a *coup d'état* to seize power. He had no rival according to family ranking, experience and government position. [Even if we were to believe the exaggerated reports by the British Political Agent in Kuwait about the rivalry between Abdullah Mubarak and Fahad, the issue was closed with the death of the latter in 1959.]

3. The process of electing a ruler becomes complicated and the family does not agree on one person, with the

probable grumbling of the Kuwaitis due to the inter-family conflict, which 'could increase the chance of a coup by Abdullah Mubarak or an outright revolution'.

4. Sheikh Abdullah Mubarak's attainment of power, either through family selection or through a rebellion. Then other Al-Sabahs request the British government to interfere, especially 'As the armed empire of Abdullah Mubarak has grown noticeably'.

5. The family selection of Abdullah Mubarak, with a serious division within, which may herald a revolution against the whole regime in the long term, or a civil war during the next five or ten years.

Those were the scenarios outlined in the Political Agent's report about the situation in Kuwait in 1958. I have been careful to cite the full text of those reports, without deletions, so that the reader might interpret the information upon which Britain designed its policy towards Kuwait and expressed its fear of Abdullah Mubarak assuming power and its consequent impact.

According to the second and third scenarios, Abdullah Mubarak could have carried out a military rebellion to seize power. According to the third and fourth scenarios, his ascendancy could have led to divisions within the family and Britain's intervention to settle the conflict, and the probability of a revolution or a civil war. The report, it seems, contradicts itself because according to these two scenarios (the third and fourth) Abdullah Mubarak's ascendancy would have taken place with the family members' consent, which should have prevented any negative consequences.

In a 1959 report, the Political Agent's assessment changed when he mentioned that the Sheikh's image had changed considerably during the past six months and that he had become more influential and generally acceptable. Therefore, the prospects of using force in the event of the Ruler's death or abdication were ruled out.[28]

A report by the US Consul on the Deputy Ruler dated 28 February 1958 reached the same conclusion. It mentioned that although no official statement was issued about Kuwait's forthcoming ruler, the consulate believed that the Supreme Council had approved the selection of Sheikh Abdullah Mubarak as Deputy Ruler. The writer based his view on discussions and information from 'reliable sources', including Bader Al-Mulla, the Emir's secretary, and Ezzat Ja'afar, the Emir's office director.[29]

British reports were full of rumours that had been circulating in Kuwait at that time, such as the claim that the conflict between the Sheikh and the Emir began in the summer of 1959 when the Ruler left to spend his summer leave in Lebanon. The reports stated that while Sheikh Abdullah Mubarak was abroad he was not requested, as usual, to return to be Deputy Ruler, which angered him. This was not true – because Abdullah Mubarak was in Sweden for medical treatment and could not return.

Another claim was that the Sheikh refused to release the expenditure statements of the Public Security Department to the World Bank for the construction and development team that arrived in Kuwait in March 1961. The team mission was to lay down the financial and accounting regulations for government departments. That was not true, either. According to the Political Agent's report dated 21 March 1961, the World Bank's mission requested all government departments, except Public Security (due to the sensitivity of its activities), to submit their proposals pertinent to the budget.[30]

Thus, the rumour that Abdullah Mubarak refused to provide the mission with military expenditure figures was baseless because the mission did not request them. Similarly, the rumour that Sheikh Abdullah Mubarak purchased weapons 'behind the Ruler's back' or without his knowledge was also unfounded. That was simply not possible because the British Government required the Ruler's explicit approval for any arms deal, as a necessary condition before the Political Agent could sign off the required licence approval for the weapon-exporting companies. In addition, the rumours about restrictions imposed by the Finance Department on armament procurements were untrue.

In fact, and in accordance with the Political Agent's report dated 19 May 1960, no major cuts were applied to the Public Security Department and the police force, as they were to the Ministry of Public Works.[31] The truth was that the Finance Department required the expenditure of current allocations before making new financial requests, and required a definitive departmental budget. Those rules were not directed against any specific department, but applied to all government departments.

According to Sheikh Sabah Al-Salem, as reported by the Political Agent, Abdullah Mubarak resigned because of criticism of the departments under his supervision. He wrote an undated letter of resignation to be handed to the Emir on or after 18 April. Abdullah Mubarak had left for Lebanon on the evening of 17 April, and the Emir therefore had no opportunity to meet him in person. After long consideration the Ruler passed the letter of resignation to the Supreme Council, asking them to submit their view.[32] After lengthy deliberations, the Council concluded on 25 April 1961 'that Abdullah Mubarak's services to Kuwait are necessary'. Sheikh Jaber Al-Ahmed and Sheikh Sa'ad Al-Abdulla informed the Ruler that the Council had decided to reject the resignation and the Council asked the

Ruler to inform Abdullah Mubarak of the decision. The Ruler demurred, instructing the Council itself to communicate its decision. The Council sent a letter to Abdullah Mubarak in Beirut requesting him to revoke his resignation and to return to Kuwait to resume his responsibilities.

Sheikh Abdullah Mubarak sent an immediate written reply, which, according to the Political Agent's report, 'was like a slap in the face'. Abdullah Mubarak thanked the Council for its letter and then explained that a discussion of his resignation was beyond its jurisdiction. The Council could not judge him: that was a matter between himself and the Emir alone.

The Emir sent a delegation to Lebanon asking him to return, but he did not. However, he did not say that he would stay abroad, and he had made it clear that he would withdraw his resignation if the Emir asked him to do so. Only that act would he regard as showing the Ruler's full personal confidence in his deputy. Abdullah Mubarak's view was based on the fact that he was the most senior member of the Council, in age and status; that he chaired the sessions in the Emir's absence; therefore, the decision to accept or reject his resignation had to be the Emir's alone.

Abdullah Mubarak did not withdraw his resignation; neither was it accepted by the Supreme Council. The Ruler did not take a decision to accept or reject it. This was an unprecedented situation in the Emiri court. Abdullah Mubarak had been the guiding light of Kuwait, the engineer of independence, for as long as most people could remember – and this impasse created a crisis in Kuwait's government.[33] According to the Political Agent in his report on 30 April 1961, he thought that Sheikh Abdullah Mubarak would shortly return to his former position but only 'after losing some of his feathers'.[34] However, 'losing his feathers' meant to Abdullah Mubarak that his judgement was now in question, at a supremely important moment in Kuwait's history. As the senior servant of the state, he would only hold office if he had the unqualified confidence of the head of state. The uncertainty continued for the whole of May and early June, with independence imminent on 19 June.

On 17 June, the Emir made a decision. He did not inform Abdullah Mubarak that he would accept the resignation, but there was a surprising parallel development. Two days before the declaration of independence, on 17 June 1961, he authorized Emiri Decree No. 7/1961:

> We Abdullah Al-Salem Al-Sabah, the Emir of Kuwait, out of our desire to coordinate work and activities and run them smoothly in realization of public interest, we decree the following:
>
> Article (1): Sheikh Sa'ad Al-Abdullah Al-Salem Al-Sabah shall be appointed Chief of Police and Public Security.
>
> Article (2): Heads of Departments should implement this Decree
>
> Emir of Kuwait
Abdullah Al-Salem Al-Sabah

That is, the Emir appointed his eldest son to the main post held by Abdullah Mubarak. On the same day, he issued Emiri Decree No. 8/1961, which introduced some changes in government departments. The Customs Department was merged with the Ports Department and would be called the Department of Customs and Ports (Article 1); the government's Domains Department was merged with the Housing Department to be called the Housing Department (Article 2). Kuwait Radio was annexed to the Supreme Council, under the name: The House of Radio and Television (Article 3).[35]

This meant that some of the departments led by Abdullah Mubarak were reorganized or merged, and were no longer under his control. Yet, the greatest 'feather' of all, the armed forces, remained firmly under his command. When analysing these changes, the Political Agent noticed that the Emiri Decree did not address the army, and that it transferred radio from the Public Security Department to the Supreme Council.[36] In the aftermath of this decree, *Al-Hayat* newspaper asked Sheikh Abdullah Mubarak to comment on what had happened. He refused.[37]

The question that has puzzled researchers and historians remains: why was Sheikh Abdullah Mubarak's resignation not announced until two days before independence? Perhaps a better question might be: was his resignation ever formally accepted? The Emiri decrees did not mention Abdullah Mubarak, they simply announced that, for administrative reasons and good government, the departments had been reorganized under new leadership. No one could say that he had been purged, since he remained in command of the armed forces, the most important role of all. Abdullah Mubarak had been consigned to a kind of limbo, convenient for the Emiri court.

Abdullah Mubarak: continuing commitments to public life

The Sheikh was close to many members of the Al-Sabah family. He was the son of Sheikh Mubarak Al-Kabir and thus became 'uncle' to almost all the Al-Sabah family. Further, given his Bedouin, desert upbringing, he remained loyal to the ethics of family solidarity and unity. As stated earlier, Sheikh Abdullah Mubarak began his public career in the 1930s under the patronage of the Ruler of Kuwait, his nephew Ahmed al-Jaber;

later he became Deputy Ruler in the 1950s under another nephew: Sheikh Abdullah Al-Salem.

Sheikh Ahmed al-Jaber had meant a great deal to Abdullah Mubarak. He was his patron, his mentor, and like a father. For more than 25 years Abdullah Mubarak's promotion in governmental posts was due to Ahmed al-Jaber's trust and encouragement. This explains the strong bonds between Abdullah Mubarak and the sons of Ahmed al-Jaber: Jaber and Abdullah. In the 1950s Sheikh Jaber, who later became Ruler of Kuwait, was responsible for security at Al Ahmadi port and worked closely with the Sheikh; his brother Abdullah was the Sheikh's deputy and trusted assistant in the Public Security Department.

Sheikh Abdullah Mubarak was always ardent in pursuit of the Al-Sabah family's status and solidarity. He acted immediately against anything that might endanger its unity or stir intra-family conflicts. This key feature of his personality was never appreciated by the British. He had great ambitions for Kuwait, which he wanted to modernize and develop very quickly. While defending his views firmly, he never thought of resorting to force to impose his views or opinions on others.

Contrary to British fears, Abdullah Mubarak thought of the army only as a shield for the country in the face of any foreign ambitions and as indispensable to building a modern state. It was not a tool to increase his political influence. Therefore, the British records that talk about a *coup d'état* reflect a clear misunderstanding of the man and of the relations within the family. The best evidence is from 1950 when Sheikh Ahmed al-Jaber passed away, or in 1960 when Abdullah Mubarak differed with the Emir over a number of political issues.

Sheikh Ahmed was very sick in his final months and left power almost completely in Abdullah Mubarak's hands. The British talk of great rivalries and conflicts at this time was, in fact, without foundation. As Sheikh Abdullah Mubarak told me, when the family met to discuss the selection of a successor to Sheikh Ahmed al-Jaber, he described Sheikh Abdullah Al-Salem as 'my father and he is more eligible than me'.

For the next 10 years, Sheikh Abdullah Mubarak was deputy to the new Ruler, Sheikh Abdullah Al-Salem, and his right hand in administering the country. Abdullah Mubarak always showed proper respect to Sheikh Abdullah Al-Salem. He did this spontaneously and naturally, following the habitual respect that he had been brought up to observe. His role and significance became more prominent during that period, due to the quiet personality of Sheikh Abdullah Al-Salem and his unwillingness to become involved with the day-to-day decisions, leaving them to Sheikh Abdullah Mubarak. A strong working relationship therefore developed between the two men. The Ruler used to travel quite often, able to count on the absolute reliability of his 'right hand' and deputy, Sheikh Abdullah Mubarak.

Reviewing the Political Agent's monthly reports documenting the dates of Kuwait's senior officials' travels reveals that Sheikh Abdullah Mubarak became Deputy Ruler for the first time in 1950, again in 1951, again in 1952 for three months, and another time in 1953 (for three months also). In 1954, he acted as Deputy Ruler for two months; in 1955 for three months; in 1956 for one month; in 1957 for four months; in 1958 for nine months (due to the Ruler's travel schedule); in 1960 for six months.

It is noticeable that during the three years before independence, the Deputy Ruler's responsibilities increased markedly. That is confirmed by many reports written by the Political Agent. I shall refer to some of the reports written during 1957–60, the period that directly preceded independence. A report written by the Political Agent on 17 January 1957 noted that the Ruler no longer threatened to resign or abdicate, but 'the periods he spent abroad were becoming longer and more frequent'.[38] In 1959, the Political Agent repeated that remark and said in his report on 11 February that: 'The Ruler ... has been visiting Kuwait from time to time, but scarcely ruling.'[39] Again in June, the Political Agent mentioned that Sheikh Abdullah Mubarak 'was Acting Ruler most of the time'.[40] In another report on 5 August, he added: 'That Ruler could fairly be regarded as living in semi-retirement in Lebanon and only visiting Kuwait from time to time.'[41]

In 1960, British reports referred to this issue several times. In the Political Agent's report dated 19 May he wrote that Abdullah Mubarak was 'the acting Ruler' for a long time.[42] On 5 June 1960 another report stated that: 'The Ruler has been absent for most of the period and whenever he is away, Abdullah Mubarak has been acting ruler.'[43] Writing in the Political Resident's Annual Report for 1960 about the conditions in Kuwait, he mentioned: 'The Ruler has continued to avoid involvement in the day-to-day intrigues inside the ruling family and among the Kuwaiti community generally, by living for the most part outside Kuwait.'[44]

The US Consulate's reports on 29 December 1957 and on 29 October 1959 reiterated the same narrative.[45] In this long-running situation, Abdullah Mubarak's loyalty to the Ruler was absolute. During the absence of Sheikh Abdullah Al-Salem, the Sheikh was keen to seek his advice by telephone on important issues before taking any decision. He made several short visits to Lebanon to meet the Emir and to discuss with him what was happening in Kuwait. Their relationship was very strong.[46]

However, in the year before Kuwait's independence, Abdullah Mubarak and the Emir had very different, if not opposing, views on a number of issues. These included the developments of the border problem with Iraq. Sheikh Abdullah Mubarak believed that Britain had no interest in solving the border problem with Iraq. Thus it followed that reliance on British diplomatic intervention would lead nowhere: he thought that Kuwait must take the initiative and engage Iraq on the issue. The continuing intervention of British officials fuelled the dispute and endlessly prolonged its term. The second issue where they differed was the new equipment for the army, which Abdullah Mubarak viewed as the shield of the country and to which, naturally, external countries were deemed a threat.

The armed forces were his special concern. He had invested enormous energy in building up the nation's defences, in particular his decision to create a small air force. He took pleasure in wearing the beret and army uniform, had amicable relationships with his officers and men, and fostered the careers of the Kuwaiti pilots who had learned to fly at the club he had sponsored. He knew that the small Kuwaiti air force would be outclassed by the much larger Iraqi air force, but he believed that his skilled pilots flying the best aircraft available would cause real damage to an attacker.

We cannot be sure why he chose the Jet Provost trainer as a ground attack or fighter plane. He made an intensive study of the available aircraft, and the most likely reason that he selected the Provost was that it would be the perfect aircraft with which to train Kuwaiti pilots to qualify on jet aircraft. Up to that point they'd had to go to Britain for jet training with the Royal Air Force. The Provosts meant that they could be taught to fly in Kuwait.

The story of his long battle to equip the armed forces has been told in Chapter 3, but it is probable that the debate over fighter aircraft may have played a part in his resignation. Four days after the Council's intervention in the matter of his private resignation, the contract for the Jet Provosts was confirmed. Then four days after independence the position was reversed and the contract was cancelled. The purchase of the Jet Provosts was a matter of great personal significance to Abdullah Mubarak, and any attempt at cancellation would have called in question his judgement, and hence his ability to remain in government.

There was also the issue of the new civil and penal codes to be adopted. Sheikh Abdullah Mubarak wanted more time for consultation and consideration of the probable consequences of these laws, so that the legislation would receive social legitimacy and the citizens' respect. For instance, he noticed that some articles of law did not reflect the social conditions and values of the Kuwaiti people and might violate the prevailing traditions and norms. Nor did they sufficiently recognize the difference between the prevailing conditions of people in the city, and those of the desert and the tribes. Abdullah Mubarak felt this matter deeply.

It is unlikely that the Emiri court politics of this crucial period can ever be unravelled, because the evidence does not exist. Or does it? While I was preparing this book, I reviewed the Political Diaries that contain reports of the British Political Agent in Kuwait. I noticed that the diaries for 25 April to 24 May 1961 and the period from 25 August to 24 September 1961 have not been declassified, although those documents were not 'top secret', and despite the lapse of over 30 years.

The rule by which documents could be restricted after 30 years is as follows: 'some records were closed for even longer than 50 years, at the request of particular government departments'. One of the criteria for extended restriction was 'international relations', while another was 'potential harm to people still alive'. Both might be pertinent in this case, but it is likely that potential damage to current British relationships with Kuwait may be the most likely cause. Whatever the cause, these documents covering a crucial period have remained inaccessible to researchers to date, but might be released on appeal. Certainly, the reason for their restriction would be the sensitivity of the information they contain.

When Sheikh Abdullah Al-Salem died in 1965, Sheikh Abdullah Mubarak returned to Kuwait to attend the funeral. After the funeral, Sheikh Sabah Al-Salem stood up and kissed the head of his uncle Abdullah Mubarak and said: 'The rule is yours, uncle.' Sheikh Abdullah Mubarak answered that he had not returned to rule. He then added, 'I trust you and bless all your choices.'

The same thing happened in 1977 when Sheikh Sabah Al-Salem passed away. Abdullah Mubarak was in Kuwait at that time, and when consultations began on selecting the ruler, some family members visited him and told him he was the most suitable candidate. But Sheikh Abdullah Mubarak rejected the idea and blessed the nomination of Sheikh Jaber Al-Ahmed as Emir and Sheikh Sa'ad Al-Abdulla as Crown Prince. This took place in the Dasman Palace and is well attested.

His concern with the family's image and prestige was no less than his preoccupation with its unity and solidarity. Abdullah Mubarak was not merely the heir of his father, but also the champion of his memory and reputation. It is no secret that Mubarak Al-Sabah had seized power from his brothers. This accusation of usurpation dogged him through his period as Ruler, causing deep rifts in the family. His son Abdullah Mubarak was a man with a high sense of honour, and had served his country selflessly. The last thing he would wish to do would be to disrupt the stability of the family, or in his own case raise the old canard about usurpation. I have shown above that although he possessed the qualities of a ruler, he always placed himself outside the contest, especially in 1950.

There is one further aspect to his resignation. Everywhere in the Gulf, British officials were obsessed with disputed and violent successions. It was their fantasy of what Arab rulers would always do. So they confidently predicted that Abdullah Mubarak would contest the accession of both Sheikh Ahmed and Abdullah Mubarak III, and cause dispute in numerous other scenarios. Now, as independence grew near, the old doubts surfaced once again. Would nothing ever end this falsehood? His task was done – independence was in sight. He had achieved his goal. Now he could wash his hands of it all and resign with a clear conscience.[47]

A final observation: Abdullah Mubarak believed that the Al-Sabah should not engage in trade or commerce. Further, he contended that politics, government and trade should never mix, and he was committed to that principle from his resignation until his death in June 1991. Such belief systems and values changed considerably in Kuwait after the oil surge, and politics became enmeshed with trade. But this was a world in which he wanted no part.

-7-

Resignation and Beyond

A bdullah Mubarak's determination to resign was neither a
hasty nor an impulsive gesture. It had many causes, some
personal and others political. Yet it is hard to tease out the
personal and psychological factors that influenced his decision,
perhaps even dominated it. For many years, his official life had
dominated his existence. Then he married, later in life than
many of his contemporaries, and hoped for a family life. After
more than 25 years of public service, he had an additional set of
priorities. For the first time, he gave priority to his personal life.

The decision to leave Kuwait was based upon this new shape
to his life. It was a retreat, for a period, to Lebanon, travelling to
Beirut in January 1961. He was careful to follow up the
negotiations with London over the aircraft deal, and continued
to fulfil the obligation of his public life. He still met regularly
with politicians and journalists, as well as holding meetings and
seminars on Arab issues.

It was only King Saud's impending visit to Kuwait that drew
him home. In April, he returned to Kuwait to receive his old
friend, because he knew the importance of showing the Al-
Sabah's solidarity and unity to their closest ally, the Saudi royal

family. He took part in the reception ceremonies during the visit and as head of the army prepared a large-scale military parade.[1] The King's sons were his guests at Mishref Palace, and he was at the centre of all the arrangements for the visit. However, despite the calm on the surface, it was not always possible to hide the underlying tensions. At one point, it was rumoured that King Saud had intervened between the Ruler and Sheikh Abdullah Mubarak,[2] but there is no firm evidence.

I clearly recall the events of the night preceding our departure from Kuwait for the second time. We were sitting in the garden of the White Palace. Night fell and Abdullah Mubarak's guests bade him farewell. He was surrounded by a number of his close personal friends and assistants who had worked with him for many years. They included Sheikh Mubarak al-Abdullah Al-Jaber, Hamad Al-Humaidhi, Suleiman Al-Mousa, Mohammed Ja-afar, Abdul Razzaq Al-Qaddoumi, Yacoub Beshara, Salem Abu Hadida and Ezzat Ja'afar. I was sitting beside Abdullah Mubarak when he called Ezzat Ja'afar to his side. He produced a sealed letter and handed it to him. He said that this was to be delivered to the Emir personally, on the next day or as soon as possible. This was the letter that precipitated the resignation crisis. He did not want to put any pressure on the Emir, so he left it undated. However, the intention was clear. He expected the Emir to accept his decision and to announce the resignation at a time that he deemed fit. There was no suggestion of any ultimatum, and he was ready to serve the Emir in any way that he wanted. That final act completed, he asked Jabra Shuhaider to prepare the aircraft for the flight to Lebanon. We left on 17 April.

We boarded the plane at 6.00 a.m. and some dear friends were there to see us off. Sheikh Mubarak al-Abdullah Al-Jaber, to whom Abdullah Mubarak had been like a father and teacher, boarded with us and tried to convince Abdullah Mubarak not to leave. Suddenly he broke down and began to weep. Sheikh Abdullah Mubarak comforted him, saying that he was leaving Kuwait in safe hands and he needed to rest.

A few days after our departure, the Emir, Sheikh Abdullah Al-Salem, sent a delegation comprising Sheikh Mubarak al-Abdullah Al-Jaber, Hamad Al-Humaidhi and Nasser Al-Sabah to Lebanon with a message requesting Sheikh Abdullah Mubarak's return. Abdullah Mubarak listened attentively to what they had to say, then answered quietly that his position was known and his views on the disputed issues would not change. Those issues were the border dispute with Iraq, the policy for arming the armed forces, and some of the clauses of the civil and penal code. He had thought long and hard about these matters and his mind was made up.

Yet when the invasion threat from Iraq came in June 1961, Sheikh Abdullah Mubarak knew that he could not remain abroad while Kuwait was in danger. He returned quickly on 27 June and expressed his readiness to work, as an ordinary citizen, anywhere. However, it was an uncomfortable visit and he felt his presence was embarrassing his friends at a time of crisis. So he returned to Beirut the next day. He then announced that the Emir had asked him to contact the Secretary General of the Arab League to co-ordinate Arab support for Kuwait.[3]

During that crisis, Sheikh Abdullah Mubarak used his close relationship with the most senior Iraqi officers to abort the plans of massing on the Kuwaiti border. The commander of the Iraqi Third Armoured Division played a major part in that initiative and later on was granted political asylum in Egypt through Abdullah Mubarak's efforts.[4]

His travels continued. In May 1962, he returned again to Kuwait in sadness to attend the funeral of his sister Sheikha

Hessa, the widow of Sheikh Salem Al-Hamoud and Sheikh Sabah's mother-in-law.[5] In June, he visited Egypt and met President Nasser.[6] In September, he visited a number of countries including Italy, Germany, Austria and Morocco.

In 1963, he visited the Vatican for an audience with the Pope. Although Abdullah Mubarak no longer held any official or government position, and although the Pope's aides asked him not to raise any political issues in the meeting, he directly addressed the subject of the Pope's forthcoming visit to Israel. He asked bluntly: was it political or religious? The Pope quickly reassured him, stressing the entirely religious nature of his visit, telling Abdullah Mubarak that going to Israel in no way signalled any change in the Vatican's attitude towards the Palestinian cause. It was a visit to the Holy Shrines.

Nevertheless, during that period, rumours continued to proliferate around Abdullah Mubarak. In December 1962, King Hussein informed the British Ambassador in Amman that he had obtained information that the Sheikh was plotting a *coup d'état*, using mercenaries, and that he was in touch with either Nasser or Qassem. This was unfounded, as the Ambassador knew. He stated firmly in the telegram he sent to London that the King's statement had no validity, and that although he was passing it to the Foreign Office he did not believe it. He did not believe there was any connection between Abdullah Mubarak and Qassem.

The Foreign Office sent the information to its embassies in Kuwait and Cairo for verification. The British Embassy in Kuwait described the information as 'improbable' and the British Embassy in Cairo said it had received no evidence to confirm it. The only outcome was that King Hussein's numerous assertions became less credible.

The truth is that Abdullah Mubarak rejected any foreign intervention or mediation between him and his brothers among the Al-Sabah. He also rejected strongly the attempts of some states that tried to exploit this conflict, or the offers (whatever intentions were behind them) to support him in restoring his position in Kuwait. He used to reiterate: 'I resigned out of my free will. I hold my record in my right hand; my role is so engraved in Kuwait's history that no one can deny it.'

In 1965, the rumour again circulated that he was plotting a *coup d'état* or intending to form a government in exile. On this occasion, Abdullah Mubarak tactfully returned immediately to Kuwait as if he wanted to say: 'I am among you and I would do nothing against my homeland, my family and my kin.' He was received warmly by Sheikh Khaled al-Abdullah Al-Salem, Sheikh Jaber Al-Ahmed, Sheikh Mohammad al-Ahmed al-Jaber and Sheikh Sa'ad al-Abdullah Al-Salem. He returned again in September because he had received bad news about Sheikh Abdullah Al-Salem's state of health. Sadly, it was to be the last time that they would meet, and Abullah Mubarak returned to Kuwait in October for his old friend's funeral.

During our stay in Beirut, our house was always busy with Kuwaiti visitors, Lebanese journalists and politicians of all ideologies. Abdullah Mubarak consistently used his political and moral influence to support President Nasser and his policies. This activity, it seems, was monitored by the Egyptian Embassy in Beirut, as reflected in the report dated 21 February 1963 entitled: 'The Activity, Inclination and Political Affiliations of Prince Abdullah Mubarak Al-Sabah.' We remained in Beirut until 1965 when we decided to move to Cairo, at the invitation of President Nasser. We were actually in Paris when we received the invitation to live in Egypt; President Nasser viewed Cairo as the natural place for Abdullah Mubarak and his family to make their home. With his deep affection for Egypt, Abdullah Mubarak greatly appreciated the offer and accepted with alacrity. We went directly to Egypt from France. At first, we lived at Khalil Agha Street in Garden City, then moved to the 'Al-Oraba Palace' in Alexandria, and finally to our long-term home in Misr Al-Jadida.

During our stay in Egypt, Sheikh Abdullah Mubarak was given the status of a foreign dignitary on all state occasions and celebrations attended by President Nasser. These included the opening of the National Assembly, the July Revolution Anniversary Ceremony and the visits of Arab heads of state. The President also used to invite him to special occasions, such as his daughter Huda's wedding in 1966, and that of his other daughter Muna later on. When Nasser died in 1970, Sheikh Abdullah Mubarak was among the first to go immediately to the family's residence at Manshiyat Al-Bakri and then to Qasr Al-Qubba. After President Nasser's death, Abdullah Mubarak's special status continued throughout President Sadat's period in office.

During those years, Abdullah Mubarak continued his active work in the wider Arab community. When the Syrian separation from the United Arab Republic occurred on 28 September 1961, he condemned the event in the Lebanese press. During Algerian Support Week in Lebanon, Sheikh Abdullah Mubarak donated 100,000 Lebanese lirat. With the Tripartite Declaration of Unity between Syria, Iraq and Egypt in 1963, Sheikh Abdullah Mubarak presented 100 jeeps to the Egyptian Army, and gave advice to President Nasser in March 1964. In 1966, he sent a cheque for US$1 million to President Nasser, 'leaving full freedom to the president to use it for any welfare purpose'; the President assigned the whole amount to the scientific colleges at Cairo University, especially Al-Qasr Al-Eini Hospital.

The Palestinian cause was always uppermost in his mind, and he worked tirelessly on its behalf, taking special interest in the Palestinian Students Union in Gaza. When the 1967 war broke out we were in Geneva. One morning Abdullah Mubarak learned of Egypt's urgent need for medical and pharmaceutical supplies. He took immediate action, working with a pharmacist of Egyptian origin to secure the immediate purchase and transportation of these vital supplies to Cairo. He also supplied a number of ambulance vehicles as well as donating 1 million Egyptian pounds to the Egyptian Army. After the Israeli invasion of Lebanon in 1982 he donated US$1 million, half of which was in the form of medicine and the other half in cash. This was sent through the International Red Cross in Geneva. During the 1973 war he donated 1 million Egyptian pounds to Egypt's military effort and continued his highly effective support for the Palestinian cause.

In 1973, we experienced terrible heartbreak; we lost our elder son, Mubarak. We were on our way from Cairo to Geneva; I was sitting with Mubarak when he had a sudden and acute attack of asthma in mid-flight. By the time the plane landed in Athens, Mubarak had passed away. We returned to Cairo and President Sadat was at the airport to receive us. His care and attention to us was extraordinary; his nobility and generosity to us in our sorrow helped us a great deal. He took part in the funeral but was also beside us in all the burial rituals. We will never forget his kindness. Sheikh Abdullah Mubarak had a school and a mosque built close to the garden where our late son, Mubarak, lay.

In the same year, I graduated from the Faculty of Economics, Cairo University, and was awarded my BA. In 1974, I left for England to pursue postgraduate study at the School of Oriental and African Studies and the University of Surrey. Thereafter, we settled in London although there were many visits to Kuwait. Abdullah Mubarak was keen to spend the holy month of Ramadan in Kuwait so we returned in 1978.

During all these years, his major sadness and pain came from the endless untruths that surrounded him. He faced them courageously, but the pain and sorrow always revived when he learnt of a fresh attempt to defame him. He found it hard to understand why people would wish to sully his reputation: what reason could they have to belittle him or discount his role in building Kuwait? Modern Kuwait had not come into being out of nothing. There were pioneers who had laid the foundations prior to independence, and he was one of them. He used to say: 'Right will prevail and Allah will reward him.' His faith in Allah was deep, secure and unshakable. It would have been easy for him to use his extensive network of journalists to refute or respond to these many allegations, yet he rejected any such idea as demeaning. He could not conceive of mounting a media campaign, as that would discredit his country and the family. Therefore he remained silent and issued no press statement about Kuwait's internal and foreign affairs during the 30 years after his resignation. Nor did he speak of the reasons for his departure from office. President Nasser recognized this honourable and dignified behaviour, and told him that he expected no less of his old and honoured friend. It was the right way to behave. One thing was certain: only a man who knew his own worth and was confident of the work that he had accomplished would respond in such a fashion.

As the years passed, he became less and less happy with the impact of vast wealth on Kuwait. He used to say: 'This is not the Kuwait that I and my generation sought to build.' He also criticized the vast increase in non-Arabs among expatriates and said: 'Such an arrangement builds neither a homeland nor an army.' He believed that a person cannot give all his work, spirit and energy to a country that is not his own. Nationality is a fundamental part of human identity, so he believed it essential to naturalize the Arabs who had lived in the country for a long time. They deserved to be Kuwaitis.

Above all, he had an unshakable belief in progress. Yet he was also saddened that the best, long-established Arab traditions had weakened and lost their meaning. When he once saw a person walking in front of his father, he said: 'Whoever does that should never expect my favour. We never knew such disrespectful behaviour.' He used to tell me time after time that oil had tarnished our morals.[7]

§

The impact of the invasion of Kuwait by the armed forces of Iraq in 1990 was unbearable for Sheikh Abdullah Mubarak. An endless trauma, day and night, he saw the world in which he had spent his childhood, youth and manhood shaking under the oppression of occupation. Although by virtue of his long experience with Iraqi regimes he did not trust the Iraqi leadership's intentions, he had never imagined that, in its arrogance and madness, military invasion would follow. Despite the shock, the Sheikh did not lose for a single moment his will to resist or his hope for liberation. He did what he deemed was his duty towards his fellow citizens and brothers, especially those trapped abroad by the occupation.

He set up a radio station in London to be the voice of Free Kuwait, carrying all the news and details about the occupied homeland to Kuwaitis in Europe. These difficult days stirred the deepest feelings of their national identity among all Kuwaitis. Massive public meetings were organized in London's Hyde Park, and in most Arab capitals, through societies and committees for solidarity with the Kuwaiti people. At the same time, Abdullah Mubarak began to look forward to the tasks to be accomplished after liberation.

His major initiative was a large seminar held in Cairo to bring together more than 70 Kuwaiti politicians and intellectuals. Representing many different strands of opinion, they planned how to meet the future challenges of reconstruction. Between 6 and 10 May 1991, this group discussed a number of working papers and research documents that addressed the issues of parliamentary life, the constitution, foreign policy, economic development strategy, the role of foreign investments, financial and currency policies, and the role of the public and private sectors. On the social level, the seminar discussed social relations in light of the experience of occupation, the demographic structure and labour force policies, the nationality and naturalization policy, women's role in society, and environmental and pollution issues.[8]

Despite his frail health during this period, Sheikh Abdullah Mubarak emphasized the pressing need to pursue far-reaching research into the development of Kuwaiti society from the social, economic and political aspects, as well as all the aspects related to its legal status and relations with Iraq. This task was accomplished by a distinguished group of professors in politics, law and sociology in a book entitled *Kuwait: from the Emirate to the State – A Study in the Origin of Kuwait, the Development of its Legal Position and its International Relations*.[9]

Abdullah Mubarak considered the invasion to be a test of the steadfastness and resistance of the Kuwaiti people and a trial of their love for the homeland. The Kuwaitis, both inside and outside the country, overcame the crisis. The Iraqi regime did not find any Kuwaiti collaborators. There was an organized popular resistance movement in which all groups and social levels participated. Kuwaitis abroad moved to mobilize Arab and world public opinion to support the cause of their homeland, with both the internal and external efforts working in harmony.

The knowledge of this constant activity towards liberation calmed him, charging him with the psychological power and will to resist sickness and pain and to cling to life. He was afraid that he might die before the liberation of Kuwait: Allah fulfilled his dream and hopes – Kuwait was liberated while he was still alive. His son's feet trod his native soil on the first day of liberation, and Sheikh Abdullah Mubarak was buried in Kuwait's soil. He did not die oppressed or defeated, but in full pride and dignity.

Envoi

Abdullah Mubarak's health began to deteriorate in the third week of April 1991 during Eid Al Fitr. He had a blood clot and stayed for two weeks in hospital. One month later, another clot struck him.

When he left hospital for the second time, his health improved. We went to Geneva and then on to London. A multitude of friends came to visit him and their presence raised his spirits, in spite of his respiratory problems.

At 2.00 a.m. (London time) on 15 June 1991 he woke up with me next to him. I asked: 'Do you want anything?' He answered: 'Allah bless you with a long life, Allah bless you with a long life', then he took a deep sigh and passed away. The heart that had endured so much could not endure any more. His death was quiet. He was dignified in his life; and so he was in his death, with his family gathered around him, reciting the Holy Qur'an until morning when the Imam arrived and washed the corpse, assisted by Abdullah Mubarak's sons, Mohammed and Mubarak. In the afternoon of the same day, a private plane carried the body to Kuwait, accompanied by Mohammed and Mubarak, my brother Sabah and some friends and relatives. Sheikh Sa'ad Al-Abdulla, the Crown Prince and senior members of the family received the body at Kuwait airport. Despite the difficult conditions in Kuwait at that time, immediately after liberation many thousands of Kuwaitis came out on the morning of 16 June to bid farewell to the man who had spent his whole life in the service of the homeland. The Emir took part in the prayer for him. He was buried at Sulaibikhat Cemetery with his Sabah brothers: Sheikh Abdullah Al-Salem and Sheikh Sabah Al-Salem. This was according to his wishes, in the heart of his liberated homeland.

What, then, remains to be said of this man in the context of history?

Sheikh Abdullah Mubarak was a statesman committed to principle. In his political views and actions he never accepted that the end justifies the means.

The place of Abdullah Mubarak in Kuwait's history is as one of those pioneers who worked and prepared for independence. He aimed, in all his efforts, to liberate Kuwait, and struggled to achieve its independence through internal reforms and external policies.

Abdullah Mubarak's name remains in Kuwait's memory as a symbol of openness to the outside world for the benefit of Kuwait. He knew the imperative need for Kuwait of harmonious foreign relations and its concomitant, open communication with the world through education, radio and other media, as well as aviation.

Abdullah Mubarak served his country for his entire life, from childhood onwards, in power and out of power. His dedication to his country never wavered. This instinctive loyalty he had learned in the desert in his first years; and as long as Kuwait's renaissance, progress and dignity continue, Abdullah Mubarak's name will be honoured.

Notes

Chapter 1 – Abdullah Mubarak: The Formative Years

1   H.R.P Dickson. *The Arab of the Desert: A Glimpse into Badawin Life in Kuwait and Saudi Arabia* (London: George Allen and Unwin, 1949), p. 27.

2   Ibid., p. 163.

3   Ibid., pp. 52–3. The author has direct experience of all these qualities in Abdullah Mubarak. In addition, as a father the Sheikh was very loving and compassionate. He was full of love and affection for his children; Mohamed, Umnia, Mubarak and Shima'a. He was never able to get over the loss of Mubarak, the first child, who passed away on 22 June 1973. He kept his sadness in his heart and dealt with this tragic loss patiently and silently.

4   Kuwait Municipality. 1980. Yasser Mahgoub, 'Kuwait: Learning from the Globalized City', in Yasser Elsheshtawy, *The Evolving Arab City: Tradition, Modernity and Urban Development* (London: Routledge, 2008).

5   Hafez Wahba, *The Arabian Peninsula in the Twentieth Century* (in Arabic) (Cairo: Committee of Authoring, Translation and Publishing, 1967), p. 80.

6   The battle took place in Al Jahra, west of Kuwait City, on 10th October 1920. It was fought between Kuwaiti and Saudi-supported forces during the Kuwait-Najd War.

7   Najat Abdul Qader Al Jassem, *Al Tatawor Al Syasi wa Al Iktisadi Lil Kuwait bayn Al Harbien 1914–1939* [The Political & Economic Development in Kuwait between the Two Wars 1914–1939] (Cairo: Dar Al Nahda Al-Arabia, 1973), pp. 147–9.

8   Robert Lyman, *Iraq 1941: The Battles for Basra, Habbaniya, Fallujah and Baghdad* (Oxford: Osprey, 2006), pp. 29–31.
9   *Al-Musawer*, 28 November 1958.
10   PRO, FO/371/91355. From Political Agency to Foreign Office, 2 September 1951.
11   Afif Al-Tayebi, *Youm fi Al Kuwait* [Fourteen Days in Kuwait] (Beirut: Al-Youm Publications, 1952), p. 18.
12   Fadel Sa'eed Aql, *Al-Kuwait Al- Hadithah* [Modern Kuwait] (Beirut: n.p., 1952), p. 34.
13   *Al-Musawer*, 11 March 1960.
14   From the Political Agency (McCarthy) to Foreign Office, 24 June 1959.
15   *Al-Musawer*, 15 April 1960.
16   Violet Dickson, *Forty Years in Kuwait* (London: George Allen and Unwin, 1970), pp. 163–8.

Chapter 2 – State-Building in Kuwait: The Role of Abdullah Mubarak

1   Mousa Hannoun Kazar Ghadban, 'Development of Rule and Administration in Kuwait – 1936 to 1962' (Ain Shams University, Master's Dissertation, 1988), pp. 192–7.
2   John Daniels, *Kuwait Journey* (Luton: White Crescent Press, 1971), p. 57.
3   From Political Agency (Pelly) to Foreign Office, 10 May 1954.
4   Interview in *Al-Musawer*, 16 May 1952, pp. 169 and 194.
5   Ibid.
6   Daniels, *Kuwait Journey*, p. 41.
7   *Al-Nuqqad*, vol. 171, 29 March 1953.
8   Ibid., May 1954.
9   Ralph Hewins, *A Golden Dream: The Miracle of Kuwait* (London: W.H. Allen, 1963), pp. 272–4.
10   From Political Agency (Bell) to Political Residency (Burrows), 1 November 1956.

11   Yousef Al-Shehab, *Regal fi Tarikh Al-Kuwait* [Men in History of Kuwait] (Kuwait: n.p., 1993), p. 51.

12   From Political Agency (Bell) to Political Residency (Burrows), 19 November 1956.

13   From American Consulate (Seelye) to Department of State, 5 November 1957.

14   From Am Consulat, Kuwait, speech by Deputy Ruler Sheikh Abdullah Mubarak Al -Sabah, broadcast over Kuwait Radio on 1 February 1959 on the occasion of U.A.R. day. Reproduced at the American National Archives. Declassified Authority KND897428 by CEP NARA date 8/30/91.

15   American Consulate (Kuwait) to Secretary of State, 4 February 1959.

16   From American Consulate (Seelye) to Department of State, 10 and 11 February 1959. Reproduced at the American National Archives. Declassified Authority KND897428 by CEP NARA date 8/30/91.

17   See the statement's text in 'Statement to the Great Kuwait People' issued by the Amir of Kuwait in Arabic, published in *Al Kuwait Al-Youm* (Kuwait Today), 4 February 1959, p. 1.

18   *Kuwait Al-Youm* (Kuwait Today), vol. 212; 15 February 1959, p. 2.

19   From Political Agency to Political Residency, 1 October 1959.

20   PRO, FO/ 371/14008. See details of 1959 events in the British documents at: From Political Agency (Halford) to Foreign Office, 5 and 11 February 1959. Report 11 February.

21   See the Consulate's commentary on this report: From American Consulate (Symmes) to Department of State, 16 November 1953.

22   From American Consulate (Symmes) to Department of State, 19 April 1954.

23   From American Consulate (Brewer) to Department of State, 14 November 1955.

24   From American Consulate (Symmes) to Department of State, 29 May 1954.

25 Ibid., 26 September 1954.

26 Ibid., 25 October 1954.

27 Memorandum of conversation about Communist Activities in Kuwait, 15 April 1955.

28 American Consulate (Brewer) to Department of State, 5 March and 10 April 1956.

29 Ibid., 15 May 1956.

30 American Consulate (Brewer) to Department of State, 26 March 1957.

31 American Consulate (Seelye) to Department of State, 27 May 1958.

32 18 July 1958. Reproduced at the American National Archives. Declassified Authority KND897428 by CEP NARA date 8/30/91.

33 *Al-Ahram* newspaper, 1 April 1959.

34 Telegram from American Consulate (Seelye) to Secretary of State, 5 April 1959.

35 From American Consulate (Seelye) to Department of State, 8 April 1959.

36 *Al-Akhbar*, 15 June 1959.

37 *Al-Ithnein* and *Al-Dunia Magazine*, 28 June 1959.

38 From American Consulate (Akins) to Department of State, 10 June 1959.

39 From American Consulate (Symmes) to Department of State, 20 January 1954.

40 From American Consulate (Seelye) to Department of State, 30 December 1959.

41 *Guardian*, 20 June 1961.

Chapter 3 – The Key Institutions of National Development

1 The General Guide for 1949, Cairo University, Library Documents, p. 19.

2 *Al-Nuqqad*, vol. 254, 28 October 1954, p. 9; *Al-Hayat* newspaper, 26 November 1954

3   Hewins, *A Golden Dream*, p. 272.

4   *Sawt Al-Sharq*, 19 April 1954, pp. 12–13.

5   From American Consulate (Seelye) to Department of State, 26 November 1957.

6   From American Consulate (Seelye) to Department of State, 8 July 1958.

7   20 April 1959. Reproduced at the American National Archives. Declassified Authority KND897427 by CEP NARA date 8/30/91.

8   From American Consulate (Seelye) to Department of State, 8 July 1958.

9   *Humat Al-Watan*, vol. 1, October 1960, p. 5.

10 From Political Agency (Jenkins) to Foreign Office, 10 May 1951; and from Political Agency (Bell) to Foreign Office (Riches), 23 April 1956.

11 From Foreign Offices (Riches) to Political Agency (Bell), 14 June 1956.

12 Visit of Sheikh Abdullah Mubarak to the United Kingdom, prepared by Gethin, 29 June 1951.

13 PRO, FO/371/91355. From Political Agency to Political Residency, 2 September 1951.

14 From Political Agency (Jenkins) to Political Residency (Hay), 31 September 1950.

15 From Political Agency to Foreign Office, 2 September 1951.

16 From Political Agency (Pelly) to Foreign Office (Barclay), 21 and 22 May 1954.

17 From American Consulate (Brewer) to Department of State, 17 July 1956.

18 From Foreign Office (Samuel) to Political Residency (Richards), 6 January 1956.

19 From American Consulate (Seelye) to Department of State, 26 November 1956.

20 From American Consulate (Seelye) to Department of State, 10 December 1958.

21 From American Consulate (Akins) to Department of State, 26 May 1959.

22 Telegram from American Embassy in London (Whitney) to Secretary of State, 12 June 1959.

23 Report by Admiralty (Head of Military Branch II), 3 February 1961.

24 From Admiralty (Botton) to Foreign Office (Hillier-Fry), 9 February 1961.

25 From Political Agency (Richmond) to Foreign Office (Beaumont), 19 February 1961.

26 From Political Agency (McCarthy) to Foreign Office (Walmsley), 24 March 1960.

27 From Foreign Office (Beaumont) to Political Agency (Richmond), 6 February 1961.

28 From Foreign Office (Beaumont) to Political Agency (Richmond), 6 February 1961.

29 From Air Ministry (Salthouse) to Foreign Office (Hillier-Fry) 30 January 1961.

30 From Polglese to Hunting Percival Aircraft Ltd. (Brown), 11 February 1961.

31 From Foreign Office (Beaumont) to Political Agency (Richmond), 13 March 1961.

32 Polglese to H.H. Abdullah Mubarak Al-Sabah, Beirut, 8 March 1961.

33 From Political Agency (Richmond) to Foreign Office (Beaumont), 14 March 1961

34 From Polglese to H.H. Sheikh Abdullah Mubarak, 22 March 1961.

35 From Political Agency (Richmond) to Foreign Office, 27 March 1961.

36 From Air Ministry (West) to Foreign Office (Walker) 30 March 1961.

37 From Political Agency to Foreign Office, 13 April 1961.

38 From Political Agency (Richmond) to Foreign Office (Beaumont), 21 March 1961.

39 From Foreign Office (Beaumont) to Political Agency (Richmond), 8 May 1961.

40 From Foreign Office to Political Agency, 23 June 1961.

41 Secret Report by Foreign Office on 'Liaison with Kuwait Armed Forces', 13 April 1959.

42 *Humat Al-Watan*, vol. 6, March 1961, p. 7.

43 From Political Agency (Pelly) to Foreign Office, 10 May 1954; Kuwait Diary, 1954, No. 4 covering the period 27 April to 27 May.

44 *Kuwait Al-Youm*, vol. 3, 25 December 1954, p. 4.

45 Political Diaries of the Persian Gulf, 1954.

46 From Foreign Office (Ewart-Biggs) to Political Agency (Logan), 11 June 1954.

47 From American Consulate (Seelye) to Department of State, 11 March 1959.

48 From American Consulate (Symmes) to Department of State, 1 October 1953.

49 From American Consulate (Symmes) to Department of State, 5 October 1953.

50 From American Consulate (Symmes) to Department of State, 20 September 1953.

51 From American Consulate (Symmes) to Department of State, 21 March 1954.

52 From American Consulate (Symmes) to Department of State, 31 August 1954.

53 From American Consulate (Seelye) to Department of State, 11 March 1959.

54 From American Consulate (Seelye) to Department of State, April and 2 June 1958.

55 From Political Agency (Bell) to Foreign Office, 28 October 1956.

56 From American Consulate (Brewer) to Department of State, 16 October 1956.

57 *Kuwait Al-Youm*, vol. 202, 7 December 1958.

58 From American Consulate (Symmes) to Department of State, 29 April 1959.

59 From American Consulate (Symmes) to Department of State, 31 August 1954.

60 Confidential Annex to Kuwait Diary No. 10, covering the period 25 September to 27 October 1956.

61 Kuwait Diary No. 11, covering the period 24 October to 20 November 1957.

62 From American Consulate (Seelye) to Department of State, 27 April 1959. The company participated in reaching this conclusion by the mistake it committed by announcing its flights between Kuwait and Europe prior to obtaining Abdullah Mubarak's approval, thus infuriating him.

63 *Kuwait Al Youm*, no. 203, 14 December 1958, pp. 14–15.

64 Hussein Khalaf Al-Sheikh Khaza'l, *Tarikh Al Kuwait Al Siyasi* [Political History of Kuwait], 5 volumes (Beirut: Dar El Hilal, 1965), vol. 2. p. 295. For the development of Kuwait's educational system, see Dr Badr El-Dinn, *Al-Khususi, Studies in Kuwait's Social and Economic History in Modern Times* (in Arabic) (Kuwait: Zat El Salasel Publication, 1983), pp. 21–75.

65 The history of education began when Kuwaitis donated the money to build the first school 'Al-Mubarakiya', named after Sheikh Mubarak, Emir of Kuwait. It opened on 22 December 1911. The school was managed financially and administratively by the Board of Merchants. Its leading teachers included the Egyptian Hafez Wahba, the well-known Kuwaiti historian Abdul Aziz Al-Rashid, Sheikh Yousef bin Homed, Sheikh Yousef Al-Quena'i and Othman Abdullatif Al-Othman. Its first headmaster was Omar Assem Al-Ezmiri. In 1936, Ahmed Shehab Eldeen became the headmaster and was succeeded by Ahmad Dhaif. In 1920, the citizens built another school, which

was named 'Al-Ahmadiah', named after Sheikh Ahmed Al-Gabir, Emir of Kuwait at the time and was run by Abdul Malek Al-Saleh, an education pioneer in Kuwait.

66 See samples of the Board's decisions, under his chairmanship in *Kuwait Al-Youm*, vol. 22, 7 May 1955, p. 6; vol. 51,10 December 1955, p. 8; vol. 54, 31 December 1955; vol. 167, 23 March 1958, p. 4; vol. 168, 30 December 1958, p. 14; vol. 266, 13 March 1960, p. 22; vol. 267, 20 March 1960, p. 19. It is worth mentioning that the Political Agent noticed Abdullah Mubarak's concern with education and reported it. From Political Agency (McCarthy) to Political Residency (Man), 23 September 1959.

67 The minutes of the meeting are in *Kuwait Al Youm*, vol. 22, 7 May 1955, p. 6

68 The minutes of the meeting are in *Kuwait Al-Youm*, vol. 51, 17 December 1955, p. 8.

69 Ibid.

70 *Kuwait Al-Youm*, vol. 51, 10 December 1955, p. 8.

71 *Kuwait Al-Youm*, vol. 54, 31 December 1955, p. 8.

72 *Kuwait Al-Youm*, vol. 232, 19 July 1959, p. 2.

73 Ibid.

74 From American Consulate (Brewer) to Department of State, 18 March 1957 and another report by Seelye, 5 November 1958.

75 *Kuwait Al-Youm*, vol. 243, 4 October 1959, p. 11 (reprinted in vol. 245 on 18 October 1959, p. 12).

76 *Kuwait Al-Youm*, vol. 265, 6 March 1960, p. 22.

77 Ibid.

78 *Kuwait Al-Youm*, vol. 267, 13 March 1960; pp. 19–20.

79 *Al-Raed*, vol. 6, October 1952, p. 71.

Chapter 4 – Redefining Kuwait's National Interest

1   From Foreign Office (Beaumont) to Political Residency (Richard), 21 June 1960.

2   From American Consulate (English) to Department of State, 8 February 1950.

3   Foreign Relations to the US, 1946, vol. 2 (Washington, DC: US Government Printing Office, 1970), p. 56.

4   Foreign Relations to the US, 1947, vol. 5 (Washington, DC: US Government Printing Office, 1971), p. 553.

5   Foreign Relations to the US, 1949, vol. 6 (Washington, DC: US Government Printing Office, 1977), p. 1566.

6   From American Consulate in Basra (Gardin, Jr.) to Department of State, 23 June 1951. Foreign Relations to the US, 1951, vol. 5 (Washington, DC: US Government Printing Office, 1982), pp. 998–1000.

7   Office memorandum regarding the political status of Kuwait, 2 March 1952.

8   Memorandum from the legal advisor on the legal status of Kuwait, 17 September 1959.

9   From American Consulate (Symmes) to Department of State, 22 December 1953.

10 From American Embassy in Beirut (Thayer) to Department of State, 24 June 1959.

11 See Collection of Special Reports 1931–1932. Efforts by the US in support of American Interests Seeking an Oil Concession from Abdullah Mubarak of Kuwait, in Foreign Relations to the US, 1932, vol. 2 (Washington, DC: US Government Printing Office, 1947), pp. 1–29).

12 Bader El-Dinn A. Al-Khususi, *Studies in the Modern and Contemporary History of the Arabian Gulf*, vol. 2 (Kuwait: Zat Al-Salasel Publications, 1988), pp. 282–4. For the American–British Rivalry over oil, see pp. 198–323.

13   Foreign Relations to the US, 1948, vol. 5 (Washington, DC: US Government Printing Office, 1975), p. 19–20.

14   From American Consulate in Basra (Noberly) to Department of State, 29 January 1951.

15   Telegram from American Consulate (Duncan) to Department of State, 9 June 1952.

16   From American Consulate (Duncan) to Department of State, 25 July 1952.

17   From Political Agency (Jenkins) to Foreign Office, 10 May 1951.

18   From Foreign Office (Rose) to Political Agency (Pelly), 26 June 1952.

19   From American Consulate (Brewer) to Department of State, 8 October 1956.

20   From American Consulate (Seelye) to Department of State, 2 October 1958.

21   From Assistant Secretary of State (Rountree) of Near East Department (Murphy), 21 May 1959, and from Department of State to American Embassy in London, 25 May 1959.

22   From British Embassy (Washington) to Foreign Office, 4 June 1959.

23   Foreign Relations of the US, 1947, vol. 5 (Washington, DC: US Government Printing Office, 1971), p. 522.

24   Memo from legal advisor (Lofitus Baker) to Secretary of State on Iraqi attack upon Kuwait, effect on the Middle East, 15 May 1959.

25   Memo from the legal advisor on the legal status of Kuwait, 17 September 1959.

26   From Political Agency (Jackson) to Political Residency (Hay), 24 September 1949.

27   From Political Residency (Hay) to Foreign Office (Burrows), 27 October 1949.

28   From Political Agency (Bell) to Foreign Office, 15 August 1955.

29 Mousa Hannoun K. Ghadban, 'Development of Government and Administration in Kuwait, 1936–1962' (in Arabic) (unpublished MA thesis, Ain Shams University, 1988), p. 200.

30 The American Consul wrote in one of his reports that, 'He showed his usual hostility to what he considers British Interference with Kuwait's internal matters. External affairs only are the proper prerogative of the British.' From American Consulate (Seelye) to Department of State, 10 June 1959.

31 From American Consulate (Seelye) to Department of State, 2 June 1958.

32 From Foreign Office (Samuel) to Political Residency (Richards), 6 January 1956.

33 Report dated 7 April 1956 (author unknown).

34 PRO, FO/371/13223. 7 November 1958.

35 From Political Agency (Bell) to Foreign Office (Riches), 23 April 1956.

36 Telegram from American Consulate (Seelye) to Secretary of State, 31 May 1958.

37 War Office, from HQ BFAB to HQ LEPG, 24 February 1959.

38 PRO, FO/371/140180. Secret report of 13 April 1959.

39 Mustafa M. Alani, *Operation Vantage: British Military Intervention in Kuwait 1961* (London: LAAM, 1990), pp. 80–97.

40 Telegram from American Consulate to Secretary of State, 31 May 1959.

41 Telegram from American Consulate to Secretary of State, 8 April 1958.

42 From American Consulate to Secretary of State, 18 July 1958.

43 From Political Agency to Political Residency, 19 March 1959.

44 From American Consulate to Department of State, 16 March 1958.

45 Top secret telegram from Political Residency to Foreign Office, 19 May 1959; and top secret telegram from Foreign Office to Political Residency, 21 May 1959.

46 Britain informed the United States of this development. Top secret telegram from British Embassy in Washington to Foreign Office, 4 June 1959.

47 Telegram from American Embassy in London (Whitney) to Secretary of State, 19 and 30 June 1959. From American Consulate (Akins) to Department of State, 24 June 1959.

48 Report from Political Residency to Foreign Office, 22 April 1959.

49 From Political Agency (Halford) to Foreign Office, 18 May 1959.

50 From American Consulate (Seelye) to Department of State, 20 May 1959.

Chapter 5 – The Challenge of Iraq

1 From Political Agency (Dickson) to Political Residency, 9 September 1932.

2 Dr Maimouna Al-Khalifa Al-Sabah, *Kuwait Under the British Protectorate* (in Arabic) (Kuwait: n.p., 1988), pp. 91 and 182.

3 Dr Jamal Z. Qassem, *Arab Gulf: A Study of its Contemporary History 1945–1971* (in Arabic) (Cairo: Institute of Arab Studies and Research, 1974), p. 155.

4 Abdullah Zalatah, *Azmat Al Kuwait A'am 1961: Safahat minTarikh Al Ela'kaat Al Iraqiya–Al Kuwait* [The Crisis of Kuwait 1961: Chapters of Iraqi–Kuwaiti Relations] (Cairo: Modern Commercial Press, 1993), pp. 21 and 25–8.

5 See Abdullah Mubarak's letter in: From Political Agency (Jenkins) to Political Residency (Hay), 19 February 1950.

6 *Al-Ahram*, 13 March 1953.

7 *Al-Ahram*, 2 May 1953.

8 *Al-Hayat*, 16 September 1954.

9 From American Consulate (Symmes) to Department of State, 27 June 1955.

10 *Al-Ahrair*, 20 October 1957.

11 *Miraat Al-Sharq*, 26 October 1958.

12   From British Embassy in Baghdad to the Political Agency in Kuwait, 19 October 1953. It is worth mentioning that the Ambassador commented by saying that such an idea would not be welcomed in London and Kuwait. According to his information, the Kuwaitis desired to preserve their independence.

13   From Political Residency (Bahrain) to Foreign Office, 22 May 1954.

14   Al-Khususi, *Dirasat fi Tarikh Al Kuwait AlHadith Al Igtama'ie wa Al Iktisadi 1913–1961* [Studies in the Economic and Social History of Kuwait in Modern Times] (Kuwait: Zat Al-Salasel Publications, 1983), p. 149.

15   From American Consulate (Brewer) to Department of State, 23 January 1956.

16   From American Embassy in Baghdad (Elits) to Department of State 2 March 1956.

17   From American Embassy in Baghdad (Elits) to Department of State 9 March 1956.

18   The text in is the American Consul's Report: from American Embassy in Baghdad (Elits) to Department of State, 24 April 1956.

19   From American Consulate (Brewer) to Department of State, March 1957.

20   From American Consulate (Seelye) to Department of State, 4 November 1957.

21   *Al-Ithnain* and *Al-Dunia* magazine, 15 December 1958.

22   *Kuwait Al-Youm*, vol. 1, 11 December 1954, pp. 4–5.

23   From American Consulate (Seelye) to Department of State, 30 September 1957.

24   *Beirut Al-Masa'a*, 15 May 1958.

25   Abd Al Fattah, *Fikrat Nameq. Seyasat Al Iraq Al Kharagiya fi Al Montiqa Al Arabiya 1953–1958* [Iraq's Foreign Policy in the Arab Region 1953–1958] (Baghdad: Publications of the Ministry of Culture and Information, 1981), pp. 280–2.

26   See the collection of telegrams and reports about this issue: A de L. Rush, ed., *Records of Kuwait 1899–1961* (London, Archive Editions, 1989), vol. 4, pp. 83–130.

27   From American Consulate to Department of State, 23 February 1958.

28   Fikrat Nameq Abdul Fattah, *Foreign Policy of Iraq in the Arab Region, 1953–1958* (in Arabic) (Baghdad: Publications of the Ministry of Culture and Information, 1981), pp. 481–3.

29   Telegram from American Consulate (Seelye) to Secretary of State, 8 July 1958. Reproduced at the American National Archives. Declassified Authority KND897428 by CEP NARA date 8/30/91.

30   11 July 1958. Reproduced at the American National Archives. Declassified Authority KND897428 by CEP NARA date 8/30/91.

31   Telegram from American Embassy (Seelye) to Secretary of State, 23 July 1958.

32   Fikrat Nameq Abdul-Fattah: *Foreign Policy of Iraq in the Arab Region, 1953–1958* (in Arabic) (Baghdad: Publications of the Ministry of Culture and Information, 1981), pp. 486–8.

33   28 August 1958. Reproduced at the American National Archives. Declassified Authority KND897428 by CEP NARA date 8/30/91.

34   *Al-Ahram*, 14 August 1958.

35   Telegram from American Consulate (Seelye) to Department of State, 23 July 1958.

36   *Miraat Al Awsat*, 26 September 1958.

37   From American Consulate (Seelye) to Department of State, 3 November 1957.

38   *Al-Ahram*, 1 April 1959.

39   From American Consulate to Department of State, 13 April 1959.

40   From American Consulate to Secretary of State, 26 March 1959.

41 20 May 1959. Reproduced at the American National Archives. Declassified Authority KND897428 by CEP NARA date 8/30/91.

42 From American Consulate to Secretary of State, 10 June 1959.

43 From American Consulate (Seelye) to Department of State, 20 May 1959.

44 From American Consulate to Secretary of State, 10 June 1959.

45 *Iraq Times*, 2 December 1959.

46 *Al-Neda'a*, 20 March 1960.

47 From Political Agency (Richard) to Foreign Office, 1 April 1961.

Chapter 6 – The Resignation of Abdullah Mubarak

1 From Political Agency (Bell) to Foreign Office, (Fry), 15 August 1955.

2 *Al Nahar*, 22 December 1953.

3 From Political Agency (Pelly) to Foreign Office, 30 November 1953.

4 For Bahrain, see Andrew Wheatcroft, *The Life and Times of Shaikh Salman bin Hamad Al-Khalifa: Ruler of Bahrain, 1942– 1961*. London, Routledge (1995). For Abu Dhabi, *With United Strength: H.H. Shaikh Zayid bin Sultan Al Nahyan, The Leader and the Nation* (Abu Dhabi: The Emirates Center for Strategic Studies and Research, 2004; 3rd edition 2013).

5 From Political Agency to Political Residency, 28 March 1941.

6 From Political Agency (Galloway) to Political Residency (Hay), 19 January 1949.

7 From Political Agency (Jakins) to Foreign Office, 21 January 1950.

8 From American Consulate (English) to Department of State, 30 January 1950.

9 Ibid.

10　8 February 1950. See Attachment No. (42). Reproduced at the American National Archives. Declassified Authority KND832922 by CEP NARA date 8/30/91.

11　Report of 8 February 1950. Reproduced at the American National Archives. Declassified Authority KND832922 by CEP NARA date 8/30/91.

12　From American Consulate (English) to Department of State, 30 and 31 January and 5 February 1950.

13　From Political Agency (Jakins) to Political Residency (Hay), 1 March 1950.

14　From American Consulate in Basra to Department of State, 1 March 1950.

15　Jamal Zakaria Qassem, *Arab Gulf: A Study of its Contemporary History* (in Arabic) (Cairo: Institute of Arab Research and Studies, 1974), p. 48.

16　From Political Agency to Political Residency, 2 September 1951.

17　*Al-Ahram, Al-Akhbar* and *Al-Jarida* on 12 October 1953.

18　From Political Agency (Pelly) to Political (Burrows), 19 October 1953.

19　*Al-Ahram, Al-Akhbar* and *Al-Jarida*, 14 October 1953.

20　From British Embassy in Baghdad (Mackenzie) to Political Agency, 19 October 1953.

21　*Al-Jarida*, 12 October 1953.

22　From Political Residency (Hay) to Foreign Office (Ross), 25 July 1952.

23　From American Embassy in London (Rend-Field) to Secretary of State, 12 October 1952.

24　From Political Agency (Pelly) to Foreign Office, (Eden) 14 February 1955.

25　From Political Agency (Bell) to Foreign Office, (Fry) 15 August 1955.

26　From Political Agency (Bell) to Political Residency 17 January 1957.

27 From Political Agency (Halford) to Foreign Office, 19 November 1958.

28 From Political Agency (Halford) to Foreign Office (Beaumont), 25 June 1959.

29 From American Consulate (Seelye) to Department of State, 28 February 1958.

30 From Political Agency (Richmond) to Foreign Office (Beaumont), 12 March 1961.

31 From Political Agency (Richmond) to Political Residency (Middleton), 19 May 1960.

32 From Political Agency (Richmond) to Foreign Office (Walmsley), 11 June 1961.

33 From Political Agency (Richmond) to Foreign Office (Walmsley), 11 June 1961.

34 From Political Agency (Richmond) to Foreign Office (Beaumont), 30 April 1961.

35 *Kuwait Al-Youm*, vol. 332, 25 June 1961.

36 From Political Agency (Richmond) to Foreign Office (Walmsley), 25 June 1961.

37 *Al-Hayat*, 20 June 1961.

38 From Political Agency (Bell) to Political Residency (Burrows), 17 January 1957. 'The Ruler has made no further reference recently to any desire to abdicate, but the periods he spends away from Kuwait are becoming longer and more frequent and it would never surprise me in the face of the burden of his responsibilities [if] he were to announce his intention of retiring permanently to his villa in Lebanon.'

39 PRO, FO/371/140081. 11 February 1959.

40 PRO, FO/371/140083. 25 June 1959.

41 PRO, FO/371/140083. From Political Agency (Halford) to Political Residency (Man), August, 1959.

42 PRO, FO/371/148927. 19 May 1960.

43 PRO, FO/371/148927. 5 June 1960.

44 Annual Report for 1960 by Political Residency (Richmond).

45 From American Consulate to Department of State, 24 December 1957.

46 29 October 1959. Reproduced at the American National Archives. Declassified Authority NND A329922 by CEP NARA date 8/24/91.

47 There was an ancient Roman, Cincinnatus, who won his victory over the enemies of Rome and immediately retired, his task accomplished. It has been said that 'Within his lifetime Cincinnatus became a legend to the Romans. Twice granted supreme power, he held onto it for not a day longer than absolutely necessary.'

Chapter 7 – Resignation and Beyond

1 Saudi Arabia's news bulletin, April 1961, p. 1.

2 *Al-Hayat*, 3 May 1961.

3 Confidential Annex to Kuwait Diary No. 7 covering the period 25 June to 24 July 1961.

4 We lived in Beirut for a period and on 29 August 1961 our first child, Mubarak was born. He filled our life with joy.

5 *Al-Youm* newspaper, 11 May 1962.

6 PRO, FO/371/156825. 10–11 June 1962.

7 His thoughts and comments were the inspiration for many of my poems and writings.

8 *Kuwait and the Challenges of the Reconstruction Phase* (in Arabic). Cairo, Research Center, Political Studies (1992).

9 Kuwait; Dar Souad Al-Sabah, 1993.

Bibliography

---◆◆◆---

Primary sources

British diplomatic correspondence
Includes reports of the British Political Agent in Kuwait and the British Political Resident in the Gulf, who was located in Bahrain. These reports are found in the Public Records Office (National Archives) in London, most of them under FO371. Another set of documents exists in the India Office.

Many of these reports were collected and published in volumes as follows:

Annual Records of the Gulf (London: Archive Publications, 1992), 6 vols.

Annual Records of the Gulf (London: Archive Publications, 1993), 6 vols.

Political Diaries of the Persian Gulf 1904–58 (London: Archive Publications, 1990), 20 vols.

Ruling Families of Arabia, ed. A. De L. Rush (London: Archive Publications, 1971), 12 vols.

The Persian Gulf Administration Reports 1873–1957 (London: Archive Publications, 1986), 11 vols.

The Records of Kuwait 1899–1961, selected and ed. A. De L. Rush (London: Archive Publications, 1989), 8 vols.

US diplomatic correspondence

US Foreign Relations. Annual reports of American diplomatic missions abroad published by the State Department since 1861.

US National Archives and Records Administration. Since 1948. Kuwait file is number D86.

Kuwaiti documents:

Al-Kuwait Al-Youm: the official Gazette of the Kuwaiti Government. Its first issue appeared on 11 December 1954 and it was published every Saturday until 30 November 1956 from when it appeared on Sunday.

Secondary sources

In Arabic

Al Berawi, Rashed, *Harb Al Petrol in Al Sharq Al Awasat* [Oil War in the Middle East] (Cairo: The Anglo-Egyptian Bookshop, 1957).

Abd Al Fattah, *Fikrat Nameq. Seyasat Al Iraq Al Kharagiya fi Al Montiqa Al Arabiya 1953–1958* [Iraq's Foreign Policy in the Arab Region 1953–1958] (Baghdad: Publications of the Ministry of Culture and Information, 1981).

Abu Hakamah, Ahmed, '*Al Kuwait fi Segelat Shareket Al Hind Al Sharkia' fi Al Kuwait Robaa' Qarn min Al Istiklal* [Kuwait, in the Records of the Eastern Indian Company, in Kuwait: A Quarter Century of Independence] (Kuwait: Kitab Al-Arabi, January 1986).

Al Akkad, Salah, *Al Isti'mar fi Al Khalig Al Arabi Al Farisi* [Colonialism in the Arab-Persian Gulf] (Cairo: The Anglo-Egyptian Bookshop, 1956).

—— *Al-Siyasah fi Al Kahlig Al Arabi* [Politics in the Arab Gulf] (Cairo: The Anglo-Egyptian Bookshop, 1965).

—— *Al-Tayarat Al-Siyasiya fi Al Khalig Al Arabi* [Political Trends in the Arab Gulf] (Cairo: n.p, 1965).

—— *Ma'alem Al-Taghieer fi Dowal Al Khalig Al Arabi* [Landmarks of Change in the Arab Gulf States] (Cairo: Institute for Arab Research and Studies, 1972).

—— *Al Petrol wa Atharouh fi Al Siyasah wa Al-Mo'gtamaa Al Arabi* [Oil and its Influence in Arab Politics and Society] (Cairo: Institute for Arab Research and Studies, 1973).

Al Asha'al, Abdullah, *Qadeyat Al Hodoud fi Al Khalig Al Arabi* [Issue of Borders in the Arab Gulf] (Cairo: Al Ahram Center for Political and Strategic Studies, 1978).

Al Ayoubi and Ayoub Hussein, *Ma'a Zekrayatena Al Kuwaitiah* [With our Kuwaiti Memories] (Kuwait: Kuwait Government Press, 1972).

Al Ada'sani, Khaled, *Nisf A'am min Al Hokm Al Niyabi fi Al Kuwait* [Half a Year of Representative Government in Kuwait] (Beirut: n.p., 1947).

Al Dahi and Khaled Khalef, *Aswar Al-Kuwait Al Thalatha* [The Three Walls of Kuwait] (Al Kuwait: n.p., 1989).

Al Feel, Mohamed, R., *Sokan Al Kuwait* [The Population of Kuwait] (Kuwait: Al Matbo'uaat Inc., 1970).

Al Gamal, Yehia, *Al Nezam Al Doustouri fi Al Kuwait* [The Constitutional System of Kuwait] (Kuwait: Kuwait University Press, 1970).

Al Gazeya, Hussein Mohamed, *Dowal Al Khalig Al Arabi Al Haditha. El'akateha Al Dawlia wa Tatwor Al Awda'a Al Syasiya Al Qanouniya wa Al Dostouriya Fiha* [The Modern Arab Gulf States. Their International Relations and the Development of their Constitutional, Legal and Political Status] (Beirut: Al Hayat Foundation Book, 1973).

Al Goghrafiya Al Tarikhiya Lil Kuwait, *The Historical Geography of Kuwait* (Kuwait: Zat Al Salasel Publications, 1985).

Al Hatem, Abdullah Khaled, *Min Hona Badaat Al Kuwait* [Kuwait Began Here] (Kuwait: Dar Al Qabas, 1980).

Al Jassem, Nagaat Abd Al Qader, *Al Tatawor Al Syasi wa Al Iktisadi Lil Kuwait bayn Al Harbien 1914–1939* [The Political and

Economic Development of Kuwait between the Two Wars 1914–1939] (Cairo: Dar Al Nahda Al-Arabiya 1973).

Al Khususi, Bader Al Dean A., *Dirasat fi Tarikh Al Kuwait Al Hadith Al Igtama'ie wa Al Iktisadi 1913–1961* [Studies in the Modern Economic and Social History of Kuwait 1913–1961] (Kuwait: Printing and Translation Inc., 1972).

—— *Dirasat fi Tarikh Al Kuwait Al Igtama'ie wa Al Iktisadi fi Al A'asr Al Hadith* [Studies in the Economic and Social History of Kuwait in Modern Times] (Kuwait: Zat Al-Salasel Publications, 1983).

—— *Dirasat fi Tarikh Al Khalig Al Arabi Al Hadith wa Al Mo'aser* [Studies in the Modern and Contemporary History of the Arabian Gulf] (Kuwait: Zat Al Salasel Publications, 1988).

Al Mouzini, Ahmed Abd Al Aziz, *Al Kuwait wa Tarikha Al Bahri Aw Rehlat Al Shira'h* [The Maritime History of Kuwait] (Kuwait: Zat Al-Salasel Publications, 1986).

Al Rashid, Abd Al Aziz, *Tarikh Al Kuwait* [History of Kuwait] (Beirut: Al Hayah Bookshop Publications, 1978).

Al Rashidi, Ahmed, ed., *Al Kuwait min Al Imara ila Al Dawala* [Kuwait: from Emirate to State] (Kuwait: Dar Souad Al Sabah, 1993).

Al Rihani, Amin, *Molouk Al Arab aw Regal fi Al Bilad Al Arabiya* [Arab Kings or Strong Men in Arab Countries] (Beirut: Scientific Press, 1925).

Al Romihi, Mohamed Ghanem, *Al Petrol wa Al Taghayer Al Igtama'ie fi Al Khalig Al Arabi* [Oil and Social Change in the Arabian Gulf] (Kuwait: Kazmah Inc. for Publishing and Translation, 1984).

Al Sabah, Maymouna Al Khalifa, *Al Kuwait fi Zhel Al Hemaya Al Bratiniya* [Kuwait under the British Protectorate] (Kuwait: n.p., 1988).

Al Semeat, Yousef M., *Al Khalig Al Arabi: Dirasat fi Ousoul Al Soukan* [The Arab Gulf: Studies in the Origins of its Population] (Cairo: The Anglo-Egyptian Bookshop, 1970).

Al Shamlan, Seif Marzouk, *Min Tarikh Al Kuwait* [Chapters of Kuwait's History] (Kuwait: Zat Al-Salasel Publications, 1986).

Al Shehab, Yousef, *Regal fi Tarikh Al-Kuwait* [Men in the History of Kuwait] (Kuwait: n.p., 1993).

Al Sobayhi, Hassan Qayed, *Ibhar fi Al Siyassa wa Al Tarikh, Al Kuwait 1756–1992* [Journeys in Politics and History, Kuwait 1756–1992] (Abu Dhabi: Al A'ssema for Information and Advertisement Services, 1993).

Al Tayebi, Afif, *14 Youm fi Al Kuwait* [Fourteen Days in Kuwait] (Beirut: Al Youm Publications, 1952).

Aql, Sa'eed Fadel, *Al-Kuwait Al- Hadithah* [Modern Kuwait] (Beirut: n.p., 1952).

Bint Abd Al Aziz, Moudi bint Mansour, *Al Malek Abd Al Aziz wa Moutamer Al Kuwait 1342 h (1923–1924)* [King Abd Al Aziz and the Kuwait Conference 1342 h (1923–1924) (Beirut: Dar Al-Saqi, 1992).

Calverley, E., *Kont Awal Tabibah fi Al Kuwait* [I was the First Physician in Kuwait] (trans. Abdullah Al Hatem), (Kuwait: Dar Al-Kutub Institution, 1968).

Dickson, H. R. P., *Al Kuwait wa Garatiha* [Kuwait and Her Neighbours], 2 vols (Beirut: Sahari for Printing and Publishing, 1964).

Hussein, Abd AlAziz, *Mohadrat a'n Al Mogtamaa' Al Arabi Lil Kuwait* [Lectures on the Arab Society in Kuwait] (Cairo: Institute for Arab Research and Studies, 1960).

Ibrahim, Hassan A., *Al Kuwait: Dirasa Siyasiya* [Kuwait: A Political Study] (Kuwait: Dar Al Bayan for Publishing, 1972).

Lorimer, J. G., *Daleel Al Khalig* [Gazetteer of the Persian Gulf] trans. Office of the Ruler of Qatar (Doha: Al Orouba Publications, 1967).

Mahgoub, Mohamed, A., *Al Kuwait wa Al Hijrah* [Kuwait and Immigration] (Alexandria: General Egyptian Book Organization, 1977).

Ma'rouf, Iskandar, *Al Kuwait: Louloat Al Khalig* [Kuwait: The Pearl of the Gulf] (Baghdad: Dar Al Tadamon Publishing Press, 1965).

Noufal, Sayed, *Al Awdaa' Al Siyasiya Li Imarate Al Khalig Al Arabi wa Ganoub Al Jazeera* [The Political Status of the Arab Gulf Emirates and South of the Peninsula] (Cairo: Institute for Arab Research and Studies, 1961).

Qassem, Jamal Z., *Al Khalig Al Arabi: Dirasa li Tarikho Al Moua'ser 1945–1971* [The Arab Gulf: A Study of its Contemporary History 1945–1971] (Cairo: Institute for Arab Research and Studies, 1974).

Rebi'e, Abdullah Fouad, *Qadaya Al Hodoud Al Siyasiya Li Al Saudia wa Al Kuwait bayn Al Harbayn Al Alamyeten* [Issues of the Political Borders of Saudi Arabia and Kuwait between the two World Wars] (Cairo: Madbouli Bookshop, 1990).

Senan, Mahmoud Bahgat, *Al Kuwait Zahiret Al Khalig Al Arabi* [Kuwait: Rose of the Gulf] (Beirut: Dar Al Kashaf, 1956).

Sheikh Khaza'l, Khalaf H., *Tarikh Al Kuwait Al Siyasi* [Political History of Kuwait], 5 vols (Beirut: Dar El Hilal, 1965).

Wahba, Hafez, *Jazerat Al Arab fi Al Qarn Al E'shreen* [The Arabian Peninsula in the Twentieth Century] (Cairo: Committee for Authoring, Translation and Publishing, 1967).

Wilkinson, John S., *Hodoud Al Jazerat Al Arabiya wa Qesat Al Dour Al Birtani fi Rasm Al Hodoud A'br Al Sahara* [Arabia's Frontiers: the Story of Britain's Boundary Drawing in the Desert] (Cairo: Madbouli Bookshop, 1993).

Zalatah, Abdullah, *Azmat Al Kuwait A'am 1961: Safahat min Tarikh Al Ela'kaat Al Iraqiya–Al Kuwaitiya* [The Crisis of Kuwait 1961: Chapters of Iraqi–Kuwaiti Relations] (Cairo: Modern Commercial Press, 1993).

In English

Al-Ani, Mustafa M., *Operation Vantage: British Military Intervention in Kuwait 1961*) London: LAAM, 1990).

Burell, R. M., *The Persian Gulf* (New York: The Library Press, 1974).

Crystal, Jill, *Oil and Politics in The Gulf: Rulers and Merchants in Kuwait and Qatar* (Cambridge: Cambridge University Press, 1990).

Daniel, John, *Kuwait Journey* (Cutton, UK: White Crescent Press Ltd, 1971).

Dickson, H. R. P., *Kuwait and Her Neighbours* (London: George Allen & Unwin Ltd, 1956).

Dickson, Violet, *Forty Years in Kuwait* (London: George Allen & Unwin Ltd, 1971).

Finnie, David H., *Shifting Lines in the Sand* (London: I.B. Tauris & Co, 1992).

Freeth, Zhara, *Kuwait was my Home* (London: George Allen & Unwin Ltd, 1956).

Hay, Sir Ropar, *The Persian Gulf States* (Washington: The Middle East Institute, 1959).

Hewins, Ralph, *A Golden Dream: The Miracle of Kuwait* (London: W.H. Allen, 1963).

Hurewitz, J. C., *Middle East Politics: The Military Dimensions* (New York: Frederick A. Praeger, 1969).

Kelly, J. B., *Arabia, The Gulf and the West* (New York: Basic Books, 1980).

Liwnhardr, Peter, *Disorientation, A Society in Flux: Kuwait in the 1950s* (Reading: Ithaca Press, 1993).

Longrigg, H. Stephen, *Oil in the Middle East* (London, 1954).

Munro, John, *Out on a Wing: the Story of Wafic Ajouz and MEA* (Beirut: Masters Publication Communication, 1986).

Rush, Alan, *Al-Sabah: History and Genealogy of Kuwait's Ruling Family 1752–1987* (London: Ithaca Press, 1987).

Winstone, H. V. F and Zahara Freeth, *Kuwait: Prospect and Reality* (London: George Allen & Unwin Ltd, 1972).

Zahlan, Rosemarie Said, *The Making of the Modern Gulf States: Kuwait, Bahrain, Qatar, the United Arab Emirates and Oman* (London: Unwin Hyman, 1989).

Unpublished dissertations

Al Sabah, Amal Al Azabi, 'Soukan Al Kuwait. Dirasa Tatbekiya fi
Goghrafiyat Al Soukan' [The Population of Kuwait. Applied
Study in the Geography of Population], a Master's dissertation
submitted to the University of Kuwait, Kuwait, 1972.

Ghadban, Mousa Hannoun Kazar. 'Tattwer Al Hokm wa Al Idara fi
Al Kuwait 1936–1962' [Development of Government and
Administration in Kuwait 1936–1962], a Masters dissertation
submitted to the Faculty of Arts, Ain Shams University, Egypt,
1988.

Saleh, Ghanem Mohamed. 'Iraq wa Al Wehda Al Arabiya min
1939–1958' [Iraq and Arab Unity 1939–1958], a PhD
dissertation submitted to the Faculty of Economics and Political
Studies, Cairo University, Egypt, 1977.

Newspapers and magazines

The book made use of a wide range of Arab newspapers and weekly
or monthly magazines. They include:

In Egypt

Al Ahram, Al Akhbar and *Al Gomhouriya* newspapers and *Al
Musawer, Akhr Sa'haa, Al Ithnein* and *Roza Al Yusuf* magazines.

In Lebanon

Al Youm, Al Nahar, Sawt Al Ahrar, Sawt Al Sharq, Al Ayam and *Al
Hayat* newspapers and *Al Sayaad* and *Sout Al Orouba* magazines.

In Syria

Al Nuqqad magazine.

In Kuwait

Al A'rabi, Al Raed and *Homat Al Watan* magazines.

Index